Televised
Presidential Debates

PRAEGER SERIES IN POLITICAL COMMUNICATION
Robert E. Denton, Jr., *General Editor*

Televised Presidential Debates

Advocacy in Contemporary America

Susan A. Hellweg, Michael Pfau,
and Steven R. Brydon

Praeger Series in Political Communication

New York
Westport, Connecticut
London

Library of Congress Cataloging-in-Publication Data

Hellweg, Susan A.
    Televised presidential debates : advocacy in contemporary America
/ Susan A. Hellweg, Michael Pfau, Steven R. Brydon.
        p.   cm. — (Praeger series in political communication)
    Includes bibliographical references and index.
    ISBN 0–275–93621–X (alk. paper). — ISBN 0–275–93622–8 (pbk. :
alk. paper)
        1. Presidents—United States—Election.   2. Television in
politics—United States.   3. Campaign debates—United States.
I. Pfau, Michael.   II. Brydon, Steven Robert.   III. Title.
IV. Series.
JK524.H396   1992
324.7'3'0973—dc20   91–28176

British Library Cataloguing in Publication Data is available.

Library of Congress Catalog Card Number: 91–28176
ISBN: 0–275–93621–X (hb.)
        0–275–93622–8 (pb.)

First published in 1992

Praeger Publishers, One Madison Avenue, New York, NY 10010
An imprint of Greenwood Publishing Group, Inc.

Printed in the United States of America

The paper used in this book complies with the
Permanent Paper Standard issued by the National
Information Standards Organization (Z39.48–1984).

10 9 8 7 6 5 4 3 2 1

Copyright Acknowledgments

The authors and publisher are grateful to the following for allowing the use of excerpts from:

Hellweg, S. A., and Phillips, S. L. 1981. Form and substance: A comparative analysis of five formats used in the 1980 presidential debates. *Speaker and Gavel, 18*, 67–76. Reprinted with permission. *Speaker and Gavel* is a publication of Delta Sigma Rho–Tau Kappa Alpha.

Martel, M. 1983. *Political campaign debates: Images, strategies, and tactics.* New York: Longman. Reprinted with permission.

Pfau, M. 1990. A channel approach to television influence. *Journal of Broadcasting & Electronic Media, 34*, 195–214. Reprinted with permission. *Journal of Broadcasting & Electronic Media* is a publication of the Broadcast Education Association.

Pfau, M., and Kang, J. G. 1991. The impact of relational messages on candidate influence in televised political debates. *Communication Studies, 42*, 114–28. Reprinted with permission. *Communication Studies* is a publication of the Central States Communication Association.

Reprinted by permission of Greenwood Publishing Group, Inc., Westport, CT, from *Rhetorical Studies of National Political Debates, 1960–1988* edited by Friedenberg, R. V. Copyright © by Robert V. Friedenberg. Reprinted with permission.

To our parents in appreciation of their love and support:

Mary Jane Hellweg and Robert D. Hellweg

Russel W. Pfau and Vivian E. Pfau

Jacqueline Brydon Beal and Robert W. Brydon

Contents

Photographs appear after page 70.

About the Series

Those of us from the discipline of communication studies have long believed that communication is prior to all other fields of inquiry. In several other forums I have argued that the essence of politics is "talk" or human interaction.[1] Such interaction may be formal or informal, verbal or nonverbal, public or private, but always persuasive, forcing us consciously or subconsciously to interpret, to evaluate, and to act. Communication is the vehicle for human action.

From this perspective, it is not surprising that Aristotle recognized the natural kinship of politics and communication in his writings *Politics* and *Rhetoric*. In the former, he establishes that humans are "political beings [who] alone of the animals [are] furnished with the faculty of language."[2] And in the latter, he begins his systematic analysis of discourse by proclaiming that "rhetorical study, in its strict sense, is concerned with the modes of persuasion."[3] Thus, it was recognized more than two thousand years ago that politics and communication go hand in hand because they are essential parts of human nature.

Back in 1981, Dan Nimmo and Keith Sanders proclaimed that political communication was an emerging field.[4] Although its origin dates back centuries, a "self-consciously cross-disciplinary" focus began in the late 1950s. Thousands of books and articles later, colleges and universities offer a variety of graduate and undergraduate coursework in the area in such diverse departments as communication, mass communication, journalism, political science, and sociology.[5] In Nimmo and Sander's early assessment, the key areas of inquiry included rhetorical analysis, propaganda analysis, attitude change studies, voting studies, government and the news media, functional and systems analyses, technological changes, media technologies, campaign techniques, and research techniques.[6] In a survey of the state of the field in 1983 by the same authors and Lynda Kaid, they found additional, more specific areas of concerns such as the presidency, political polls, public opinion, debates, and advertising to name a few.[7] Since the first study, they also noted a shift away from the rather strict behavioral approach.

Today, Dan Nimmo and David Swanson assert that "political communication has developed some identity as a more or less distinct domain of scholarly work."[8] The scope and concerns of the area have further expanded to include critical theories and cultural studies. While there is no precise definition, method, or disciplinary home of the area of inquiry, its primary domain is the role, processes, and effects of communication within the context of politics broadly defined.

In 1985, the editors of *Political Communication Yearbook: 1984* noted that "more things are happening in the study, teaching, and practice of political communication than can be captured within the space limitations of the relatively few publications available."[9] In addition, they argued that the backgrounds of "those involved in the field [are] so varied and plurist in outlook and approach, . . . it [is] a mistake to adhere slavishly to any set format in shaping the content."[10] And more recently, Swanson and Nimmo call for "ways of overcoming the unhappy consequences of fragmentation within a framework that respects, encourages, and benefits from diverse scholarly commitments, agendas, and approaches."[11]

In agreement with these assessments of the area and with gentle encouragement, in 1988 Praeger established the Praeger Series in Political Communication. The series is open to all qualitative and quantitative methodologies as well as contemporary and historical studies. The key to characterizing the studies in the series is the focus on communication variables or activities within a political context or dimension. Scholars from the disciplines of communication, history, political science, and sociology have participated in the series.

I am, without shame or modesty, a fan of the series. The joy of serving as its editor is in participating in the dialogue of the field of political communication and in reading the contributors' works. I invite you to join me.

Robert E. Denton, Jr.

NOTES

1. See Robert E. Denton, Jr., *The symbolic dimensions of the American presidency* (Prospect Heights, IL: Waveland Press, 1982); Robert E. Denton, Jr., and Gary Woodward, *Political Communication in America* (New York: Praeger, 1985, 2nd edition, 1990); Robert E. Denton, Jr., and Dan Hahn, *Presidential communication* (New York: Praeger, 1986); and Robert E. Denton, Jr., *The primetime presidency of Ronald Reagan* (New York: Praeger, 1988).

2, Aristotle, *The politics of Aristotle*, trans. Ernest Barker (New York: Oxford University Press, 1970), p. 5.

3. Aristotle, *Rhetoric*, trans. Rhys Roberts (New York: The Modern Library, 1954), p. 22.

4. Dan Nimmo and Keith Sanders, "Introduction: The Emergence of Political Communication as a Field," in Dan Nimmo and Keith Sanders, eds. *Handbook of political communication*, (Beverly Hills, CA: Sage, 1981), pp. 11–36.

5. Ibid., p. 15.

6. Ibid., pp. 17–27.

7. Keith Sanders, Lynda Kaid, and Dan Nimmo, eds. *Political communication yearbook: 1984* (Carbondale, IL: Southern Illinois University, 1985), pp. 283–308.

8. Dan Nimmo and David Swanson, "The Field of Political Communication: Beyond the Voter Persuasion Paradigm," in David Swanson and Dan Nimmo, eds., *New directions in political communication*, (Beverly Hills, CA: Sage, 1990), p. 8.

9. Sanders, Kaid, and Nimmo, p. xiv.

10. Ibid., p. xiv.

11. Nimmo and Swanson, p. 11.

Series Foreword

Upon the birth of the technology, television was heralded as the ultimate instrument of democracy. It was, as no other medium, destined to unite us, educate us, and, as a result, improve the quality of actions and decisions of the polity. As the primary source of timely public information, television provides the greatest potential for understanding ourselves, our society, and even the world.

As early as 1964, Marshall McLuhan predicted that television would break down national barriers and transform the world into a global village. By the 1980s, some claim television would become the vehicle of direct democracy (Naisbitt, 1982, pp. 159–61; Toffler, 1980, pp. 416–32). Today, as notions of freedom and liberty spread throughout Eastern Europe and the Pacific Rim, television serves as the instrument of unification and definition.

We tend to forget that television also serves as an instrument of power and control (Innis, 1964, 1972), Quite simply, to control television content is to control public perceptions and attitudes. In America, television has become the primary medium and tool of both political campaigning and governing, culminating in the presidency of Ronald Reagan (Denton, 1988). Can television serve democracy?[1]

Without undertaking a philosophical discussion of democracy, one can identify several critical characteristics of a democratic form of government and consider television's impact in light of those features of democracy. The notion of *accountability*, for example, is essential to the notion of democracy. Because citizens delegate authority to those who hold office, politicians are answerable to the public for all actions and deeds. Elections are just one method of accountability. In America, news journalism serves as another check on political power and authority.

Television increases the accountability of politicians when it enhances public awareness and decision making. But the medium of television has been co-opted by politicians as an instrument of advocacy. Politicians surround themselves with media professionals who advise ways of nurturing the proper image, persona, or personality. It is very easy for politicians to manipulate media access and control. Thus, television is more beneficial for politicians as a medium of self-promotion.

Information is critical for citizens to make informed judgments and evaluations of elected officials. Television news is the prime source of information for the public (Kaid and Davidson, 1986, p. 185). Incomplete or inaccurate information can lead to bad public decisions. More important is the impact of the medium on the presentation of political information. Television, as a medium, especially tends to reduce abstract or ideological principles to human, personal components. Political issues and actions are linked to individuals. We have choices not among policies but between actors. As the public becomes even more reliant on television as a source of political information and the medium increasingly simplifies the information, the ability to recognize, perform, and appreciate complex social issues will also decline.

A free marketplace of ideas is vital to a thriving democracy. Diversity of thought and respect for dissent are hallmarks of the values of freedom and justice. When multiple viewpoints are heard and expressed, the common good prevails over private interest. With the advent of cable, the number of media outlets continue to increase but the diversity of programming does not, especially hard news and public affairs programming.

Remember that in America the mass media are, first of all, businesses. They require audiences to make money and turn a profit. Ratings are of great concern to news personalities and news programming is very expensive. The product of journalism is not ideas, but news (Entman, 1989, p. 11). Politicians and journalists have separate and distinct motives, neither of which contributes to the genuine exchange of philosophies or ideas. In fact, news journalists and politicians need each other. The result is an act of symbolic engagement. According to Christopher Arterton, it is like watching a tennis match without the benefit of actually playing the game (1984, p. 25). As spectators to the spectacle, we have lost access, control, and involvement in the process of democracy which leads us to the final element of consideration.

Democracy is a process of what Dennis Thompson (1987, 3) calls "collective deliberation" on disputes of issues and fundamental values. It is the national and public debate that determines the collective wisdom and will of the people. Ironically, however, as the speed of communication and information increases, political delegation and representation become less satisfying. Citizens become directly involved in the day-to-day affairs of state by watching television news. The stress of citizen involvement has moved from action to reaction, from initiator to responder.

This new form of politics has resulted in the living room becoming the voting booth (McLuhan, 1964, p. 22). The privatization of politics has made us passive observers rather than active participants in the political process. We may watch debates but seldom engage in them. As citizens, we no longer deliberate and debate. At best, through television we have established a plebiscitary democracy where mass public opinion is sovereign. Collective wisdom, however, is not the same as collective opinion. The speeding up of counting votes and opinions does not address the quality of those votes and opinions.

Within this broad context, Susan Hellweg, Michael Pfau, and Steven Brydon investigate the impact of television on presidential debates. For the authors, presidential debates have become uniquely television events. To argue that television simply transmits the debates into the privacy of our homes is naive. Television dictates the structure, format, and presentation of presidential debates; these dictates play an important role in how candidates exercise influence in the debates and how the public perceives and responds to them. To understand contemporary political debates, therefore, one must understand how television communicates and exercises influence in the creation and presentation of debates.

Hellweg, Pfau, and Brydon provide a valuable addition to the study of presidential debates. They integrate contemporary television media theory and research with existing and new research on presidential debates. They go beyond description to theory building and explanation. By tracing how presidential debates have evolved as a function of the participation of the broadcast industry, the authors examine how debates are structured to meet the demands of the medium, how candidate messages are tailored to the medium, how candidate messages are visually defined through the medium, and the consequential impact of mediated presidential debates. Thus, while several books have been written on presidential debates, this is the first to provide an integrated approach combining theory and research in television influence with current research on political debates.

Rather than some vibrant democratic exercise, presidential debates have become joint television appearances or joint press conferences with little true candidate engagement. The authors recognize that the future of presidential debates lies with the idiosyncracies of individual campaigns. Thus, the question becomes how presidential debates can best inform the electorate and serve democracy.

Is "teledemocracy" the twenty-first century's equavalency of fifth century B.C. Athenian democracy, or do we risk "telefacism?" The answer, of course, is somewhere between those extremes. Without being too deterministic, one can argue that television has changed the fundamental nature, structure, and function of American politics. The medium influences who runs, who is elected, the nature of democracy, as well as presidential leadership and the institution itself.

Perhaps we need, as Martin Levin (1980) argues, to return to a "politics of institutions, not men." This means a greater role and recognition of the other branches of government. Policy making is a collective affair rather than a competitive endeavor.

We need to also have a greater understanding of the role, function, and power of the media in our society. As social and scientific technology rapidly increases, we must carefully plan for their usage within the context of democratic values. Walter Cronkite suggested in a 1989 speech at the University of South Dakota,

> We could benefit by a journalism course for consumers. If we would teach people how to read a newspaper, how to listen to radio and watch television . . . we could create an understanding of media, of the individual strengths and weaknesses of each medium. We could lead them away from a dependence on television, back to good newspapers, magazines, and books.

Finally, civic responsibility and initiative should once again become a keystone of social life which surely transcends the nature and use of any medium. Instead of viewing *politics* as talk, maybe we should view politics as *people engaged in talk*. It must be person to person.

Jeffrey Abramson and his colleagues advocate a "communitarian conception of democracy" which would reverse the "centralization of politics and political communication" that has been the case with television (1988, pp. 24–26). The goal is to use television and all the new media for the "common good" of the citizens. The key difference is interaction, community participation in debate at the local level. It is what they call the "electronic commonwealth" where the goals of the media are to inform and to empower the people.

In the end, perhaps the answer is reflected in the wisdom of Al Smith: "The only cure for the evils of democracy is more democracy."

Robert E. Denton, Jr.

NOTE

1. This argument is based on Robert E. Denton, Jr., "Primetime Politics: The Ethics of Teledemocracy," in *Ethical dimensions of political communication*, Robert E. Denton, Jr., ed. (New York: Praeger, 1991), 91–114.

REFERENCES

Abramson, Jeffrey, F. Christopher Arterton, and Gary Orren. 1988. *The electronic commonwealth*. New York: Basic Books.

Arterton, Christopher. 1984. *Media politics*. Lexington, MA: Lexington Books.

Cronkite, Walter. 1989 Acceptance Speech for the 1989 Allen H. Neuharth Award for Excellence in Journalism, October 27. Pamphlet. University of South Dakota.

Denton, Jr., Robert E. 1988. *The primetime presidency of Ronald Reagan*. New York: Praeger.

Entman, Robert. 1989. *Democracy without citizens*. New York: Oxford University Press.

Innis, Harold. 1964. *The bias of communication*, Revised Edition. Toronto, Canada: University of Toronto Press.

Innis, Harold. 1972. *Empire and communication*, Revised Edition. Toronto, Canada: University of Toronto Press.

Kaid, Lynda, and Dorthy Davidson. 1986. "Elements of videostyle." In Kaid, Lynda, Nimmo, Dan, and Sanders, Keith (Eds.), *New perspectives on political advertising*. Carbondale, IL: Southern Illinois University Press.

Levin, Martin. 1980. "A Call for a Politics of Institutions, Not Men." In Davis Vincent (Ed.), *The post-imperial presidency*. New York: Praeger.

McLuhan, Marshall. 1964. *Understanding media*. New York: New American Library.

Naisbitt, John. 1982. *Megatrends*. New York: Warner Brothers.

Toffler, Alvin. 1980. *The third wave*. New York: Bantam.

Thompson, Dennis. 1987. *Political ethics and public office*. Cambridge, MA: Harvard University Press.

Preface

Televised debates between the nominees of the two major parties have become standard fare in contemporary presidential election campaigns. In recent campaigns for president, debates are considered a major communication event. Kathleen Jamieson and David Birdsell (1988, pp. 5–6) observe: "'Debate' has become a buzzword for 'serious politics'. . . . When debates are announced, movement in the polls slows; in anticipation, the electorate suspends its willingness to be swayed by ads and news."

Yet, televised debates among presidential candidates are not simply communication events; they are *uniquely television events*. They are broadcast to a mass audience, most of whom view them in the privacy of their own homes. Televised political debates have moved to what Susan Drucker terms "electronic public space," and because the nature of debate changes with the context, this shift has produced "a new form of debate" (1989, pp. 7, 20).

Ironically, television, the communication medium for modern debates, has been largely overlooked. Instead, media professionals and academics have continued the longstanding tradition, which dates to classical Greek and Roman oratory and was institutionalized in the American democratic tradition, of stressing the content of debates. The emphasis is placed squarely on what the candidates *say* in debates. Hence, in assessing candidate effectiveness in debates, media analysts in their commentary, and debate scholars in their more considered analyses, tend to focus on the specific arguments raised, the quality of reasoning and documentation for claims, whether participants answered the questions asked by the panelists, the amount of clash with the opponents' claims, and, of course, gaffes. Even the scoring of debates is drawn from the academic debate model, emphasizing reasoning, evidence, analysis, and refutation, in addition to delivery.

It is our position that the verbal content of presidential debates is important, and we deal with it in this volume. But we also maintain that television has altered the very nature of presidential debates in a profound fashion. Yet, as academics and interested citizens, we have not adjusted to this "new form of debate" to which Drucker refers. As Sidney Kraus (1988, pp. 7, 20) observes, "Despite the growing influence of television . . . [we have] failed to seriously investigate the role of the media in electoral politics."

We argue that the demands of television have dictated the structure and formats of contemporary debates and that the visual content of presidential debates plays an important role in the way that candidates exercise influence in televised debates. Television manifests a unique symbol system, which fundamentally shapes what is communicated to receivers, apart from the content, and has changed the very nature of presidential debate discourse. Contemporary television is not simply the direct transmission of some live event to the privacy of our own homes. Nor is it radio with pictures. Television is "a medium with its own stylistic requirements and communicative facilities" (Jamieson, 1984, p. 21). As a result, what works in a live presentation will not necessarily work on television. Television communicates in the intimate confines of a viewer's home, which demands a "cooler, more conversational" approach (Jamieson, 1988, p. 44). Also, what works on radio will not necessarily work on television. "Radio forces the listener to visualize. Television intrudes into the home of the viewer with its own images" (Nesbit, 1988, pp. 165–66). As a result, one study indicates that television exercises influence in a manner more similar to interpersonal communication than to radio, print, or traditional public address communication (Pfau, 1990).

This book employs a television perspective to investigate the sponsorship, formats, nature, and impacts of presidential debates, integrating contemporary theory and research about the television medium and influence with extant research on debates. The book will examine how presidential debates have evolved as a function of the active participation of the broadcast industry, how debates are structured to fit the demands of the television medium, how candidates' verbal messages have to be tailored to the medium, how candidates' visual messages are defined through the medium, and the persuasive effects of mediated debates.

We approach this book as scholars interested in the broad area of communication, sharing a common fascination with the specialty of political campaign communication, particularly with televised presidential debates. We acknowledge those scholars whose writings contributed to our understanding of presidential debates and the manner that television has shaped contemporary debates, especially Kathleen Hall Jamieson, Sidney Kraus, and Robert Tiemens. We add, however, that any shortcomings of this volume are ours and not theirs.

We would like to express our appreciation to Praeger for its support of the book and commitment to publishing works in political communication. We are particularly grateful for the support and assistance of Robert Denton, general editor of the Praeger Series in Political Communication, and Anne Davidson, the Sociology/Communications editor, as well as John Roberts, project editor, and Clare Wulker, copy editor, for their attention to detail in the production phase of the book. Finally, we thank Gregory Ghio for assisting us in the preparation of the manuscript.

Televised
Presidential Debates

Chapter One

History of Television Involvement in Presidential Debates

We should see debates for what they are, the only chance voters have to get a close-up look at those who might be President, unfiltered by the media or advertising agencies.

— Political Commentator Edward J. Rollins
(1988, p. 1)

Debates offer an imperfect but valuable chance for a mass audience to try to distinguish image from reality.

— Political Commentator George J. Church
(1984b, p. 31)

The role of the broadcasting industry in presidential debates has been vital to their initial development and institutionalization, ensuring that candidates have participated in them and making candidates accessible to voters through them. This role has changed substantially as debates have evolved, primarily through regulatory effects. The first broadcast debate occurred on radio on May 17, 1948, from Portland, Oregon, between Republicans Thomas Dewey and Harold Stassen in connection with the state primary. This one-hour encounter featured 20-minute opening statements and 8½-minute rebuttals from the candidates. It focused on a single issue, the question of outlawing communism in the United States, with Stassen taking the affirmative and Dewey the negative (Ray, 1961). This nationally broadcast debate drew an audience estimated between forty and eighty million listeners (Jamieson & Birdsell, 1988, p. 90).

1952 PRESIDENTIAL CAMPAIGN

In what might be called a precursor to televised presidential debates as we know them, Democratic and Republican contenders (or representatives) participated together in a nationally televised forum from the League of Women Voters convention at the Taft Auditorium in Cincinnati on May 1, 1952. The participants were Democrats Averell Harriman, Robert Kerr, and Estes Kefauver, and Republicans Harold Stassen and Paul Hoffman, representing Republican Dwight Eisenhower. The event was developed by the League with the assistance of NBC and *Life* magazine. On the basis of citizenry-based data gathered prior to the debate, the participants were asked two questions, one dealing with ways to prevent government "dishonesty and inefficiency" and the other focusing on whether to increase or decrease foreign economic aid ("5 Candidates Call," 1952, p. 13).

1956 PRESIDENTIAL CAMPAIGN

On May 21, 1956, the first nationally televised intraparty debate was broadcast by ABC from Miami. It featured Democrats Estes Kefauver and Adlai Stevenson in a one-hour encounter hosted by Quincy Howe eight days prior to the Florida primary.

In 1959 Congress amended Section 315 of the Communications Act so that broadcasters would be exempt from the requirements of the equal time provision for all political candidates, given that four conditions would be met: (1) it was a "bonafide newscast," (2) it was a "bonafide news interview," (3) it was a "bonafide news documentary," and (4) it represented "on the spot coverage of bonafide news events" (Martel, 1983, p. 174).

1960 PRESIDENTIAL CAMPAIGN

Hubert Humphrey and John Kennedy engaged in the only candidate debate during the 1960 primary season. This one-hour West Virginia Democratic debate was held, without an audience in the facility, in Charleston on May 4, 1960. Shown in Virginia and throughout the East Coast, the event was set up by the *Charleston Gazette* and a statewide television network spearheaded by WCHS-TV (Kilpatrick, 1960, p. 1).

During the 1960 presidential campaign, four general election debates were held between Democrat John Kennedy and Republican Richard Nixon after Senate Joint Resolution 207 temporarily suspended Section

315 of the Communications Act of 1934 for presidential and vice-presidential candidates (Zapple, 1979, p. 58). (See the Appendix for a chronological outline of the general election debates and their formats.) According to Theodore Windt, "even more than influencing the outcome of the election, the 1960 debates established both the precedent and format for subsequent debates" (1990, p. 1).

The four one-hour Kennedy-Nixon debates were all nationally broadcast from television studios and moderated by television news broadcasting personnel; they involved both broadcasting and print media specialists as panelists, primarily the former. CBS and NBC each sponsored one of the events, while ABC sponsored two. An attempt to impose the 1948 format failed because the candidates thought the debates would draw little interest and because no single issue prevailed in the campaign over others. Each debate provided for rebuttals but no follow-up questions. Opening and closing statements, as well as limited subject matter, were featured in the first and fourth debates. Accounts of the first debate have argued that the television viewers of the encounter gleaned different impressions of the candidates than did the radio listeners. This was due to Nixon's pallid complexion, use of a gray suit against a similarly colored background, refusal to wear makeup, and weight loss after hospitalization, in stark contrast to John Kennedy's youthful and athletic appearance (see, for example, Kirkpatrick, 1979; Mazo, Moos, Hoffman & Wheeler, 1962; Mickelson, 1972; Siepmann, 1977; Tiemens, 1978; and White, 1961). More recently, however, David Vancil and Sue Pendell (1987) have contested the viewer-listener disagreement allegations through a review of available documentation of the event.

1964 PRESIDENTIAL CAMPAIGN

Lyndon Johnson's position in the presidential race in 1964 eliminated the need for him to debate Barry Goldwater (Germond & Witcover, 1979). Likewise, 1964 represented the only presidential campaign year since 1956 without a single primary season debate (Swerdlow, 1988).

1968 PRESIDENTIAL CAMPAIGN

Robert Kennedy and Eugene McCarthy engaged in a single Democratic primary debate in San Francisco on June 1, 1968, as part of the "Issues and Answers" series on ABC. Held in connection with the California primary, the program featured three ABC broadcasters in the role of panelists. The debate enforced no time limits and the two contenders were permitted to interrupt one another (Murphy, 1990). As Jamieson and Birdsell have argued, by incorporating the broadcast within the framework of the regular ABC news interview program, the network "circumvented the requirement that if one candidate is given time, all must be given time" (1988, p. 111).

In 1968 Nixon believed he could avoid debating with Hubert Humphrey, since in early September he was leading his opponent by as much as twelve points in the Gallup poll (Germond & Witcover, 1979).

1972 PRESIDENTIAL CAMPAIGN

In the 1972 primary season, a 90-minute Democratic debate involving George McGovern, Edmund Muskie, Vance Hartke, Sam Yorty, and Edward Coll was televised on March 5 from the University of New Hampshire in Durham. In this debate, which featured no candidate cross-examination, local newsmen queried the contenders (Witcover, 1972, p. 1). While a Florida primary debate involving Muskie, Humphrey, McGovern, John Lindsay, and George Wallace was planned in Miami for March 13, the event was cancelled when the Muskie campaign registered an objection to the format and Humphrey argued that the debate might be "divisive to the party" ("Two Candidates Foil," 1972, p. 36).

Three more Democratic televised debates were held during the campaign season, one hour each, in connection with the California primary. For these debates, as in 1968, news interview shows were employed as broadcast vehicles, the first on "Face the Nation" (CBS) between Hubert Humphrey and George McGovern on May 28, the second on "Meet the Press" (NBC) between these same two candidates on May 30, and the third on "Issues and Answers" (ABC) involving Hubert Humphrey, George McGovern, Shirley Chisholm (in New York), Sam Yorty, and a representative for George Wallace (Taylor Hardin) on June 4. As noted by Kurt Ritter and Susan Hellweg, the difficulties involved in staging these three debates illustrated "the tendency of the 'equal time rule' to discourage presidential primary debates," specifically the events associated with nonmajority candidates attempting to participate in them (1986, p. 3). While Humphrey and McGovern initially agreed to the series of debates and engaged in the first two, a federal court appeal by Shirley Chisholm forced the inclusion of the other three in the last encounter.

In 1972 Nixon again did not perceive pressure to debate his Democratic opponent, George McGovern, who was "politically wounded by his own missteps" (Germond & Witcover, 1979, p. 193).

The Aspen Institute decision in 1975 radically changed the role of broadcasters in the coverage of debates and subsequently affected the sponsorship and location of the 1976 presidential campaign debates, as well as the participation of broadcasters as moderators or panelists in them. The Aspen Institute specified that broadcasters could be exempt from equal time provisions for debates if five conditions were met: (1) that they were set up by a third party (not affiliated with a broadcaster), on the assumption that in this way they would not be both making and covering the news; (2) that the events would take place outside of a broadcasting studio; (3) that they would be covered live, so as to safeguard their newsworthiness; (4) that they be covered in their entirety, so as to preclude the potential for biased editing; and (5) that they be centered around "good faith journalistic judgment of the newsworthiness of the event," and not be inclined toward the political interests of any single candidate (Martel, 1983, p. 174).

1976 PRESIDENTIAL CAMPAIGN

With the 1976 presidential campaign debates, the League of Women Voters stepped into the role of a sponsor of these events. Between February and May 1976, the League sponsored four Democratic presidential primary campaign debates which were nationally televised. These debates were cast as regional forums (New England forum: February 23, 120 minutes, involving Birch Bayh, Jimmy Carter, Fred Harris, Henry Jackson, Milton Shapp, Sargent Shriver, and Morris Udall; Southern forum: March 1, 90 minutes, involving Carter, Jackson, and Shapp; Mid-Atlantic forum: March 29, involving Carter, Frank Church, Harris, Jackson, and Udall; and Mid-West forum: May 3, 60 minutes, involving Church and Udall). Essentially, these forums set the stage for regular televised presidential debates during the primary season. Using a specific political theme for each debate (employment, inflation, energy; social security, welfare; urban issues; defense, detente, trade), these events were held in a community location, as opposed to a broadcasting studio, and utilized subject-area experts as panelists, rather than journalists. The same journalist served as the moderator for all four debates.

Sixteen years after the Kennedy-Nixon debates took place, general election presidential debates were resumed with three 90-minute presidential encounters featuring Democrat Jimmy Carter and Republican Gerald Ford, and one 75-minute vice-presidential encounter involving Democrat Walter Mondale and Republican Robert Dole.

Among the prominent features of the 1976 debate formats were follow-up questions, rebuttals, and closing statements. These events, like their primary counterparts, were sponsored by the League of Women Voters and held in community locations. However, in this case, print and broadcast media journalists served as panelists, primarily the former, and as moderators, primarily the latter. In contrast to the 1960 debates, live audiences were permitted for the 1976 general election debates, though no audience reaction shots were permitted during the debates themselves.

The first of two significant media-related incidents associated with the 1976 debates was the twenty-seven-minute audio gap during the first Carter-Ford meeting, where the television media faced the decision as to whether to stop transmitting the event or to stay with it; this decision was affected, of course, by the 1975 ruling relative to the media's role in covering such events as opposed to creating them (see Lang & Lang, 1984). The second significant incident was the Ford miscue about Soviet domination of Eastern Europe in the second debate with Carter; audience perceptions of the miscue did not become totally crystallized until after media interpretations of the event (see Steeper, 1980). This gaffe probably served to heighten candidate fears of losing control in debates, and to strengthen candidate perceptions that a tightly structured format, with little left to chance, must be sought after.

According to Robert Friedenberg (1990), the 1976 election campaign was pivotal in three respects in institutionalizing candidate debates. First, Ford initiated the participation of an incumbent (albeit unelected) president in debates, countering the argument that an incumbent candidate cannot risk giving the opponent credibility through the debating process or debating issues of foreign policy as this might put the nation at risk. Second, when Carter ran for re-election in 1980, it was difficult for him to avoid debating, because he had engaged in three such encounters in 1976. Third, 1976 marked the initiation of vice-presidential debates.

1980 PRESIDENTIAL CAMPAIGN

The 1980 presidential campaign featured five televised Republican primary debates between January and April and two general election debates, the first between Independent John Anderson and Republican Ronald Reagan and the second between Democrat Jimmy Carter and Reagan. For the primary debates, the notion of subject-area experts as panelists was abandoned. Three of the five televised primary debates were sponsored by the League of Women Voters, another by the *Des Moines Register*, and another by the University of South Carolina and the *Columbian Record*.

Print media journalists were employed as panelists almost exclusively for three of the primary debates; for the other two primary debates, no panelists were utilized. For four of the five debates, broadcasters acted as moderators, while for the remaining debate a print media journalist served in this role. Possibly the most significant event, from a media perspective and certainly from a candidate strategy perspective, was the Reagan "control of the microphone" incident. During a local debate in Nashua, New Hampshire, the incident involved the inclusion of other candidates besides himself and George Bush; it was covered by the media subsequent to the debate itself and proclaimed Reagan a commanding candidate (see Martel, 1983).

For the two 1980 general election debates, all but one of the panelists were print media journalists (the exception being a broadcaster). The moderators in both cases were broadcasters. These League of Women Voters–sponsored events were held in community locations. The first of the two 90-minute debates, of course, represented the only time that (1) a minor party candidate has participated in a general election debate and (2) one of the major party candidates was absent.

The Reagan-Anderson debate lasted 60 minutes and featured six main questions (no follow-up questions), candidate rebuttals, and closing statements. The Carter-Reagan debate lasted 90 minutes, and allowed for eight main questions, follow-up questions, and closing statements. A particularly notable format feature in this debate was the use of two rebuttals for the candidates in each round.

In 1981, the Federal Communications Commission (FCC) ruled to allow debates to be televised from broadcasting studios for "technical convenience," as long as a "qualified" sponsor had arranged the event (Martel, 1983, p. 174). On November 8, 1983, the FCC announced a ruling which significantly altered the sponsorship of future debates. Much against the objections of the League of Women Voters, the FCC ruled that radio and television stations could stage debates involving candidates of their own choosing without violating equal time provisions (Ritter & Hellweg, 1986). An effect of this ruling was the proliferation of Democratic presidential primary debates in the next election campaign and the growth in the variety of sponsors involved in convening these events.

1984 PRESIDENTIAL CAMPAIGN

During the pre-primary and primary season for the 1984 presidential campaign, fourteen Democratic debates were televised nationally, regionally, and locally between October 1983 and June 1984 (Ritter & Hellweg, 1986) through commercial network, cable, and public broadcasting outlets. Ironically, while both CBS and NBC sponsored two of these events, ABC sponsored none. The CBS broadcast on March 28, 1984, represented the first network-sponsored debate since the McGovern-Humphrey series of primary debates in 1972 (Ritter & Hellweg, 1986). Among the other sponsors for the primary debate telecasts were the League of Women Voters (four), the *Des Moines Register*, the *Boston Globe*, WNBC-TV in New York, and for the first time, a number of independent organizations, namely the Harvard Institute of Politics and the Massachusetts Citizens Coalition for Arms Control, the U.S. House of Representatives Democratic Caucus, the Iowa Farm Unity Forum, and the Chicago Bar Association (Hellweg, 1984; Ritter & Hellweg, 1986).

These debates tested a variety of formats, almost entirely dispensing with traditional panelists. Television news anchors or commentators were often the moderators (e.g., Tom Brokaw, John Chancellor, Ted Koppel, Dan Rather, Sander Vanocur, and Barbara Walters), and an informal format was generally used to stimulate discussion, as opposed to panelist questions (Hellweg, 1984). Community facilities, including universities, were employed by and large for these debates.

The two presidential debates between Republican Ronald Reagan and Democrat Walter Mondale and single vice-presidential debate between Republican George Bush and Democrat Geraldine Ferraro were sponsored by the League of Women Voters. For all three events, the moderators were broadcast and print media journalists, primarily the latter. The two presidential debates were 100 minutes and 90 minutes in length, respectively. The first focused on domestic policies and the second on foreign policy. The 90-minute vice-presidential debate was split between foreign and domestic subject matter. All three debates featured follow-up questions, candidate rebuttals, and closing statements.

Reports from the deliberations of two national study groups on presidential debates in 1985 and 1986 significantly affected the sponsorship of these events in 1988. First, the bipartisan Commission on National Elections was established by the Center for Strategic and International Studies at Georgetown University in February 1985. Co-chaired by Melvin Laird and Robert Strauss and comprised of forty representatives from the media, business, public service, labor, and public interest organizations, the Commission recommended that (1) presidential debates be institutionalized and (2) the two major political parties assume responsibility for ensuring that their nominees would participate in such events by securing their commitment prior to their nominations. Included with the report was a Memorandum of Agreement on Presidential Candidate Joint Appearances signed by the chairmen of the Republican and Democratic National Committees, Frank Fahrenkopf and Paul Kirk, two members of the Commission.

Second, a study group was assembled in December 1986 at the Harvard University Institute of Politics, sponsored by the Twentieth Century Fund. Chaired by Newton Minow and comprised of thirty participants and observers of past debates, it recommended that (1) presidential debates be institutionalized to prevent speculation as to whether there would be debates from taking over the focus of the campaigns themselves and (2) the two major parties jointly establish a nonprofit, bipartisan organization to coordinate the development and execution of these events.

Much to the opposition of the League of Women Voters, on February 18, 1987, the chairmen of the two major parties announced the formation of the Commission on Presidential Debates, a body whose purpose was to sponsor both presidential and vice-presidential debates commencing with the 1988 campaign. Co-chaired by Fahrenkopf and Kirk, the ten-member Commission laid the foundation for three presidential debates and one vice-presidential debate in the fall.[1]

1988 PRESIDENTIAL CAMPAIGN

Whether due to these events or not, the 1988 presidential campaign witnessed the proliferation of debates, with nearly triple the number of primary debates in 1984, and the continuation of a wide variety of debate sponsors. Without an incumbent in the race, both Democrats and Republicans engaged in televised debates, primarily the former. The first prime time televised debate during the 1988 presidential race occurred on July 1, 1987, thus initiating such encounters much earlier than ever before. These televised debates were almost exclusively covered by cable and public broadcasting outlets. Only one national network offered a debate, NBC, on December 1, 1987 (during prime time); this particular debate, prior to the official primary/caucus season, involved both Democrats and Republican candidate segments on foreign and domestic policy (alternating order), and was moderated by Tom Brokaw. The League of Women Voters sponsored two back-to-back Democratic and

Republican debates in February, just prior to the New Hampshire primary, plus a Democratic debate in New York in April.

Print media sponsors included the *Des Moines Register* (as in 1980 and 1984) for both Republican and Democratic debates; the *Dallas Morning News* and the *Texas Monthly* (in conjunction with KERA-TV) for both Republican and Democratic debates, and the *Atlanta Journal* and the *Atlanta Constitution* for both Republican and Democratic debates. Community sponsors included the League of Iowa Municipalities for a Democratic debate; the Brown & Black Coalition for a Democratic debate; the Iowa Farm Unity Coalition, the League of Rural Voters, and the Prairiefire Rural Action organization for a Democratic debate; the Roosevelt Center for American Policy Studies (in conjunction with WLS-TV) for a Democratic debate. Political organizations sponsoring televised debates included the Democratic Leadership Council for several Democratic debates and state party organizations.

Broadcasting organizations also played a role in the arranging of some of these debates: the National Association of Producers and Television Editors (NAPTE) for a Democratic debate, and the Radio/Television News Directors Association (RTNDA) (in conjunction with Iowa Broadcasting and KRTA-Radio) for a Democratic debate. Moderators in these debates were generally nationally recognized broadcast journalists (e.g., Ken Bode, Tom Brokaw, William F. Buckley, John Chancellor, Linda Ellerbee, Edwin Newman, Roger Mudd, and Judy Woodruff), with exceptions occurring in some of the community-sponsored forums where a key representative played this role. When panelists were utilized (not often), they sometimes consisted of journalists, although on a few occasions they were members of the opposite political party (a new feature in the 1988 primary debates). Universities were among the community locations employed for these debates.

The two presidential debates between Republican George Bush and Democrat Michael Dukakis and single vice-presidential debate between Republican Dan Quayle and Democrat Lloyd Bentsen were sponsored by the Commission on Presidential Debates. As early as July 7, 1987, the Commission on Presidential Debates had announced that it would sponsor general election debates on September 14 (Annapolis), September 25 (Wake Forest), October 11 (Pittsburgh), and October 27 (Omaha). On July 1, 1988, the League of Women Voters also announced the sponsorship of general election debates on September 8 (Birmingham), October 6 (Minneapolis–St. Paul), October 23 (Boston), and November 1 (Los Angeles).

Prior to the three debates which eventually took place, a sixteen-page Memorandum of Understanding was generated by representatives of Bush and Dukakis, outlining the conditions under which presidential and vice-presidential debates could be held. (In 1984 a Memorandum of Understanding developed in conjunction with the League of Women Voters—though not signed by its representatives—was only three pages in length.) This document was presented to the potential sponsors of these debates. Outlined in this document were (1) the number of debates; (2) their dates, locations, and times; (3) their sponsorship (the Commission for the first two debates and the League of Women Voters for the third debate); (4) the selection and role of the moderator and panelists; (5) the specific questioning pattern and the use of closing statements; (6) time restrictions; (7) candidate address form; (8) the use of notes; (9) the staging (camera placement); (10) microphones; (11) the height of the podiums; (12) camera shot limitations; (13) the use of tally lights and the color of the backdrop; (14) the use of green-amber-red signal lights; (15) audience control; (16) ticket distribution and seating arrangements; (17) the use of makeup specialists; (18) candidate opportunities for technical briefing sessions; (19) the use of dressing rooms/holding rooms; and (20) the use of aides and security personnel.

On October 3, 1988, the League of Women Voters withdrew its sponsorship from the second presidential debate, scheduled for ten days later in Los Angeles, arguing against the terms stipulated in the Memorandum of Understanding presented to them on September 28. Additional stipulations of the candidates to the Memorandum of Understanding consisted of an open-ended financial agreement for the debates (to be assumed by the League), the provision of a telephone line to the moderator via the producer from the campaign representatives during the debate, plus particular backdrop and rug specifications for the debate staging (Harian, 1988).

In a statement made to the press on October 3 by its president, Nancy Neuman, the League argued on principle that the campaigns were taking over the events, "the campaigns had determined what the television cameras could take pictures of . . . had determined how they would select those who would pose questions to their candidates . . . had determined that the press would be relegated to the last two rows of supporters . . . had determined the format" (League of Women Voters, 1988, p. 2). A League press release described the agreement as a "closed-door masterpiece." To the League, a point of particular concern about the agreement was the lack of opportunity for follow-up questions. Interestingly, eight days later CBS issued a statement from Dan Rather indicating that he would "prefer to report on the process than participate in it," pulling out of a panelist role in the second presidential debate, saying that "the procedures they have developed are not the best" (Sharbutt, 1988, p. I11).

The League had drawn up a proposal in May 1988 (as they had in May 1984) for a moderator-only format. A *Washington Post* story ("Dates Set," 1988) reported that Dukakis was willing to participate in a moderator-only format; however, Bush's representative, James Baker, indicated that they would only consider it if a 60-minute debate format were utilized rather than a 90-minute one. The Dukakis camp then turned down the proposal, putting the League proposal out of the negotiation process.

In a study providing an in-depth analysis of forty-six newspaper editorials resulting from the League's decision to withdraw from the second presidential debate, Madeline Fish found five categorical themes. Eight editorials argued in support of the League's decision, but also contended "that the show must go on" (1989, p. 10). Two editorials offered support for the League's position, but also expressed the belief that good could result from the outcome by "the Commission on Presidential Debates taking the League's criticism to heart or from a sincere effort by party leaders to educate voters" (pp. 10–11). The largest group, consisting of twenty-six editorials, indicated support of the League's decision to withdraw, but also suggested that the voters were the big losers. Three editorials were labeled by the researcher as being not only supportive of the League but also angry. Seven editorials were characterized as being unsupportive of the League. According to the researcher, only one of the forty-six editorials examined had nothing favorable to say about the League and its decision to withdraw from the debate.

One year after the general election, the League of Women Voters commented retrospectively on their withdrawal in a presentation before the Speech Communication Association convention, saying,

Our refusal last year to sponsor a debate should not be seen as a decision to end once and for all our involvement in political debates or our concern for their future visibility. . . . The League has no vested interest in debates, other than that they meet our institutional goal of promoting an informed electorate. (League of Women Voters Education Fund, 1989, p. 6)

The three 1988 general election debates, all sponsored by the Commission, featured identical formats (no opening statements, no follow-up questions, opportunities for single rebuttals), a broadcasting specialist moderator, three media panelists (two print media specialists in the first debate, two broadcasters in the second and third debates). The two presidential debates were held at universities; the vice-presidential debate was held at a civic center facility. Both foreign and domestic policy issues were raised in the debates, with a clear distinction drawn for these segments in the first debate only. In comparison to previous general election debates, these three encounters featured the following: (1) no follow-up questions (only the 1960 debates, the 1976 vice-presidential debate, and the 1980 Reagan-Anderson debate had not featured them); (2) no reaction shots of opposing candidates solely in the camera frame (only two-person shots from the side were provided); and (3) boisterous audience reaction to candidate comments (due to the increased percentage of party representatives over community representatives).

THE FUTURE OF PRESIDENTIAL DEBATES

Debate Sponsorship

The sponsorship issue in connection with presidential debates remains unresolved. The primary debates seem destined to be sponsored by a variety of groups. At this level, experimentation of formats is easily achieved and negotiation of terms seems less likely to be contested. Candidates are more willing to take risks in these events. Debate sponsorship at the general election level revolves around at least five contenders.

The Television Networks. The national television networks have successfully hosted presidential debates on occasion; specifically, they sponsored the four 1960 presidential debates (CBS, NBC, ABC) before the League of Women Voters stepped into the role, primary debates in 1968 (ABC) and 1972 (CBS, NBC, ABC) through weekly news interview programs, two primary debates in 1984 (CBS, NBC), and one primary debate in 1988 (NBC) through special broadcasts.

Tom Brokaw (1987) argues that the networks' news divisions have "no ideological drum to beat," that "journalism is the common forum for making choices" (1987, p. 74) and in covering the political conventions the networks have proven themselves in providing fair and accurate analysis of the proceedings. Douglass Cater counters this argument by saying that "sponsorship by the networks would confuse their role as reporters rather than managers of political events and would create incentives to exploit the debates for maximum entertainment value" (1987, p. 87).

Brokaw states that he would not be opposed to joint sponsorship of these events by the networks and the American Society of Newspaper Editors or by individual networks and individual newspapers; in so doing, he presents the case of cooperation between networks and newspapers in conducting national surveys (i.e., CBS and the *New York Times*, NBC with the *Wall Street Journal*, and ABC with the *Washington Post*).

Brokaw further makes his case by citing the two 1984 primary debates hosted by Dan Rather on CBS and himself on NBC, saying "The single moderator format facilitated a coherent, continuous line of questioning" (1987, p. 74). While Brokaw does not suggest that the single moderator format is the only way to conduct a debate, he does argue for the successful quality of these particular debates because they were sponsored by networks. Finally, Brokaw comments on the power of the networks to see that debates take place, suggesting that they would not be pushed around by candidates and their managers, and that if a candidate were to refuse to debate, the network could choose to televise a discussion with the opponent.

Joel Swerdlow (1984) contends that the networks have the necessary technical expertise and adequate financial resources. He further argues that since debates are staged solely for television (e.g., they are timed to the second to coincide with broadcast schedules), the networks are a logical sponsor. Like Brokaw, Swerdlow believes that the networks would possess more power than other potential sponsors in getting the candidates to participate in debates, since these events can only be broadcast by the networks.

On the negative side, Swerdlow points to a possible conflict of interest with network sponsors because they are not public service organizations but profit-making entities. In their effort to attract and satisfy a large quantity of viewers, Swerdlow argues, the networks might be tempted to "prepare for, promote, and stage debates that maximize the buildup, the excitement, and the drama—and to equate good debates with good television" (1984, p. 49). A case in point, Swerdlow contends, would be the use of audience reaction shots, the networks favoring them in the interests of journalistic freedom and the candidates likely not favoring them because of any possible inference about candidate performance. Another concern expressed by Swerdlow is the question of what television networks would do with third-party candidates. Newton Minow and Clifford Sloan (1987) point to the fact that because the networks do not have a formal relationship with candidates, the institutionalization of presidential debates does not become possible. Neuman and Harian argue that "network sponsorship of debates would leave American voters even more vulnerable to the already far-reaching influence of the broadcast media on presidential campaigns and elections" (1987, p. 78). This influence, the authors contend, is felt in decisions the media makes about which candidate campaign events to cover, "handicapping" of candidates as the campaign progresses, their involvement in candidate advertising time decisions, their reporting of public opinion surveys they have commissioned, and endorsement of political candidates.

Swerdlow (1984) brings up the question of how the networks as debate sponsors would cover their own performance, specifically how they would provide coverage on the debate negotiations of which they were a part or on the workability of the format used in a debate which they arranged. Other journalistic institutions, argues Swerdlow, may be logical choices as debate sponsors because their job is to inform the public, but they would not necessarily be capable of securing candidate commitment to participate.

The Political Parties. Democratic party organizations at the state level and the Democratic Leadership Council frequently sponsored primary debates during the 1988 presidential campaign. Minow and Sloan contend that the political parties are "the most likely vehicle for institutionalizing debates" (1987, p. 70) because of their ongoing relationship with the candidates. Cater counterargues by stating that the "political parties would not dare negotiate the debates in good faith until the major party nominees had been selected and had staked out their personal strategies" (1987, p. 87).

Swerdlow (1984) points out that parties would enhance their role in American political life by sponsoring debates. However, he also contends that the parties would not force their candidates to participate in a debate that would lessen the chances of winning. Bipartisan sponsorship of these events, he adds, would shut out third-party contenders. Neuman and Harian argue that party-sponsored debates "could be little more than political pillow fights, with no referee—no honest broker—representing the public" (1987, p. 79).

Jamieson and Birdsell argue that "if any single force in American politics can institutionalize debates it is political parties" (1988, p. 212). They further contend that sponsorship by the parties would enhance party identification with candidates. On the negative side, the researchers point to the fact that because the party nominee controls the party machinery and selects the party chair, he maintains control over the debate situation. Like Swerdlow (1984), they also recognize the exclusion of third-party candidates in debates sponsored by the political parties.

The Congress. The House Democratic Caucus sponsored a primary debate during the 1984 presidential campaign. Swerdlow (1984) maintains that the U.S. Congress should sponsor the debates, arguing that "Congress could make it extremely difficult—if not impossible—for candidates to play self-serving games about when and under what circumstances they would consent to a debate" and that "Congress could best guarantee the most unbiased debate arrangements" (1984, p. 83). Cater counterargues by stating that "Congress has neither sought such sponsorship nor is likely to go against the strategies of the two major candidates" and that "its members are not in session and are otherwise electorally engaged during the campaign season" (1987, p. 87).

Swerdlow contends that "members of Congress would provide continuity and high levels of public trust" to the debate process. He suggests that either the Senate or House of Representatives could invite the major nominees to address them jointly, perhaps with a panel of congressional leaders posing questions to them or with the contenders answering questions put to them by floor members. Swerdlow argues that Congress would gain prestige by such sponsorship and the political parties would be strengthened by the process; he also believes that holding such events on Capitol Hill would evoke "images of presidential addresses to joint sessions of Congress" (1984, p. 56).

The League of Women Voters. The League of Women Voters has sponsored nine general election debates (1976, 1980, 1984) and fourteen primary debates (1976, 1980, 1984, 1988), ten among Democratic contenders and four among Republicans. The League can be credited with institutionalizing vice-presidential debates (1976, 1984) and with providing a general election debate with a major-party candidate (Reagan) alongside a minor-party candidate (Anderson). As noted by Neuman and Harian, the League is the only organization to have sponsored presidential debates in three consecutive primary and general election campaigns. The early developmental history of League sponsorship of presidential debates is well documented by Peggy Lampl (1979) and Warren Decker (1981).

Neuman and Harian, representing the League of Women Voters, argue that this body can "offer persistent pursuit of the public interest under all political circumstances" (1987, p. 77) as a nonpartisan organization whose "chief objective is to help citizens cast informed votes" (1987, p. 78). While Cater believes the League has "demonstrated the most valid experience in managing very difficult negotiations" and has acted as an "honest broker" in the past, the League "lacks the enduring authority to assert primacy over all other competing claimants" (1987, p. 87).

The candidates, according to Neuman and Harian, have been the beneficiaries of the proliferation of debate sponsors in recent history, allowing them "the opportunity to shop around for the best possible—in other words, the safest—debates" (1987, p. 78), at the expense of the public interest.

Swerdlow (1984) points to two problems with League sponsorship of presidential debates. The first is a perpetual problem, that of fund raising, and the second is that of continuity between top officials in the League as new ones come in and others are replaced.

The Commission on Presidential Debates. The relatively newly formed bipartisan Commission consists of ten directors, an executive director, and a fifty-member advisory board; its mission is to sponsor debates and educate voters (Carlin & Brown, 1989; Prentice, 1988). According to Diana Prentice, the Commission has no interest in sponsoring primary debates; rather, it is positioning itself to be the sponsor of general election debates. Its vision for debate sponsorship was noted in a statement incorporated in the 1988 general election debates program: "an historic commitment by the two political parties to institutionalize the debates. . . . its mission is to instill a new spirit in American politics—a spirit that reflects the caliber of the Lincoln-Douglas debates" (Carlin & Brown, 1989, p. 4). Prentice contends that the League's withdrawal from the second 1988 presidential debate likely damaged its credibility in gaining sponsorship for 1992 debates and that the "Commission's success in fund raising and in handling the technical aspects of sponsoring debates has put it in good stead for 1992" (1988, p. 14).

Frank Donatelli and Leslie Francis (1987) suggest that three factors can explain the apparent shift in control from debate sponsor to the candidates themselves since 1960: (1) candidates recognize that debates will not take place without them, thus they will not participate without consideration of their self-interests; (2) as the importance of fall campaign debates have been historically established, candidates are increasingly careful that all of the negotiated concerns coincide with the strategies of their campaign; and (3) as the proliferation of debate sponsors has occurred, the leverage of an individual sponsor has declined. This suggests that the candidates will have much to say about the outcome of the current debate over presidential debate sponsorship.

Swerdlow (1984) believes that a debate sponsor must be considered fair by both the candidates and the public. He contends that the sponsor needs not only to be viewed as an "honest broker" but also as nonpartisan. The League of Women Voters in the past has been able to persuade those involved that it has these qualities, has been notably successful in negotiating terms for four cycles of presidential debates, and has dealt with difficult and perhaps controversial decisions (e.g., the question of including John Anderson in the 1980 general election debates). The Commission on Presidential Debates invited the League to serve in an advisory capacity to it; the League declined (Prentice, 1988). The contest over debate sponsorship appears to exist primarily at the general election level. The Commission and the League seem to be the principal contenders. Whether the Commission can bypass the criticisms associated with party sponsorship of debates and whether the League will suffer long-term effects from its withdrawal in 1988 remains to be seen.

The Inescapability of Presidential Debates

Presidential debates have nearly become an institutionalized part of the campaign landscape. The public has come to expect them. The primary debates have given American politics a variety of formats with which to experiment. Growth in the number of intraparty debates has been accompanied by a widening of potential sponsors for these events, such that a single debate does less to "make or break" a candidate's standing in the race as a result of gaffes. Swerdlow (1984) notes also that a growing deregulatory sentiment "has prompted the weakening and dissolution of federal equal-time restraints on the broadcast of debates," making it easier for these events to occur. The growing emphasis on the importance of the primary campaign has additionally focused increased attention on the need to debate as the race develops at the intraparty level.

From the candidate's perspective, as campaign costs continue to skyrocket, it would stand to reason that debates ought to become an increasingly important vehicle to reach voters. Early concerns about how to logistically deal with a minority candidate in general election debates (e.g., John Anderson), how an individual from an incumbent administration (e.g., Ford, Carter, Reagan, Nixon, Mondale, Bush) could participate in debates without relinquishing national policy secrets, and whether a sitting president (e.g., Ford, Carter, Reagan) would even appear in such events have by and large been laid to rest.

While the future of presidential debates may lie with the idiosyncracies of individual campaigns, certainly the momentum exists to make them an inescapable component of intraparty and interparty campaign processes. Precedents set by other candidates, decreased regulatory inhibitors, and public expectations about these events suggest that debate participation is inevitable. The question then becomes how the debates or joint appearances can best inform the electorate through formats on which all parties can agree.

NOTE

1. This material was derived from an information circular entitled "Background of the Commission," which can be obtained from the Commission on Presidential Debates, 1825 I Street NW, Suite 400, Washington, DC, 20006.

Chapter Two

The Structure of Presidential Debate Formats

The goal is not to find a "perfect" format for presidential debates, but rather to develop appropriate and productive ones for different situations.
—Communication Professor Susan Hellweg
(1984, p. 25)

The perfect format may never be devised or even accepted by the candidates, but any debate format produces more opportunity to address issues than do advertising, stump speeches, or evening news sound bites.
—Communication Professor Diana Prentice Carlin and Executive Director of the Commission on Presidential Debates Janet Brown
(1989, p. 1)

Any serious candidate for president of the United States . . . will be able to avoid revealing anything about his positions he does not wish to reveal. This will hold true no matter how skillful or tough a question is asked, and no matter who asks it; most politicians of national stature can evade uncomfortable questions by emphasizing unrelated points. Thus, whatever the format, only the candidates ultimately determine the quality and depth of information provided to voters.
—Journalist Joel L. Swerdlow
(1984, pp. 20–21)

According to J. Jeffery Auer (1977), traditional debate contains the following five elements: (1) a confrontation, (2) in equal and adequate time, (3) of matched contestants, (4) on a stated proposition, and (5) to gain an audience decision.

Looking at the prerequisite conditions of debate described by Auer, it is doubtful whether presidential campaign debate telecasts thus far have measured up to these conditions. As a result, even designating these events as debates is questionable. Stated propositions, for example, have been largely absent from these events; there has been little direct candidate confrontation evidenced in most of these encounters. These events, in fact, have often been referred to as "joint television appearances," rather than debates.

Many problems inherent in political debates and their coverage make it difficult to overcome many of the criticisms levied against current political debate forums. Adapting a traditional model of debate, such as that suggested by Auer, to modern technology is problematic at best. The public, being accustomed to slick, brief presentations through television, a medium highly oriented toward entertainment value, would be resistant to more lengthy discourse characteristic of the Lincoln-Douglas debates. Jamieson and Birdsell have argued "The televised debates of the past two and a half decades have been shaped by the assumption that their audience has a short attention span and is drawn to the event by the prospect of clash" (1988, p. 98).

Furthermore, political candidates are inherently comfortable with a press conference format. It is a context that they are familiar with in everyday campaigning. As a result, this is the format that generally has been utilized in past presidential debates. Employing any other type of format becomes risky to candidates. Therefore, changes in present formats are difficult.

Unfortunately, debates do not serve the public well when they simply encourage candidates to score against one another, rather than actually debate. The problem has been exacerbated by formats that have made the events somewhat akin to boxing matches, with the emphasis on scoring and avoiding a knock-out blow. In the same vein, the media has often relied heavily on a winner-loser orientation in describing debates. Evidence of this tendency is clearly provided by a study conducted by Jane Blankenship and Jong Geun Kang of the print media's coverage of the 1984 general election debates. Through their examination of stories, editorials, and cartoons in ten major newspapers covering the debates, they identified three broad metaphorical themes: war and aggression, sports, and showbiz. According to the researchers, the first theme, war and aggression, was reflected in the statements that the candidates "assailed, assaulted, and attacked each other . . . battled, beat up, blasted, bloodied, and blew each other away . . . bruised, jolted, jousted, pounded away, tussled, lit into and socked it to each other" (1991, pp. 308–9). Likewise, they found the sports theme in a number of baseball and boxing metaphorical references to "the longball . . . late inning collapse . . . best of five series . . . first game at Wrigley Field . . . heavyweight championship fight . . . ring judges" (1987, p. 5). Finally, the researchers noted the showbiz theme in references to such terms as *actor*, *performance*, *script*, and *lines* (1987, p. 6).

Another problem in presidential debates cited by Lloyd Bitzer and Theodore Rueter (1980) is that the formats utilized encourage short answers, leading to the resounding of "worn commonplaces" heard frequently in the campaign. While intended perhaps to be amusing, an October 24, 1988, *Newsweek* cartoon by James Borgman made an important statement. Here the reader saw five campaign aides heading into campaign headquarters for a debate briefing, each carrying a suitcase. The first suitcase was labeled "Spontaneous Quips Writer"; the second, "Candid Asides Writer"; the third, "Indignant Retorts Writer"; the fourth, "Memorable One-liners Writer"; and the fifth, "Closing Remarks Writer" (p. 17). The cartoon called attention to the prepacked rhetoric characteristic of debates. Still, while the candidate may benefit by packaged "commonplaces" by being able to deliver messages rapidly in polished form using various tested appeals, the public does not really gain much more than they otherwise have acquired from commercials and campaign stump speeches. Echoing this sentiment, Meadow maintained that "the debates offer candidates an opportunity to offer prepared remarks of the whistle-stop variety under the guise of a debate" to journalists' relatively predictable questions (1983, p. 91). He further argued that "debates take on the characteristics of television game shows rather than forums for high-level discourse" (1983, p. 100).

The role of panelists in presidential debates, as well as their selection (e.g., Henry, 1984) has been a source of difficulty. When panelists pose propositions from which contenders can develop arguments, then true debate occurs. The tendency in past presidential debates has been for the panelists to enter somewhat of a third-party role, taking up quite a bit of time in asking questions, directing some hostility toward the candidates in the content of their questioning, and choosing questions that do not invite debate. On a few occasions, these questions have seemed more a reflection of the interest of a particular panelist than the interests of the candidates or the public.

Panelists also have frequently been guilty of asking multiple questions within the framework of a single question, making it difficult for a candidate to respond. The panelists have often been observed pressuring the candidates with hostile or one-sided questions into submissive responses, acting as though their role was to unmask the candidates (e.g., when Dan Quayle was asked three times in the 1988 vice-presidential debate what he would do as president). The debates have often seemed more like press conferences than debates, with panelists asking questions of candidates, and candidates responding to the questions, rather than debating one another. In a study of the 1980 presidential debates, Jeffrey McCall (1984) in fact made particular note of the pseudo debate between the panelists and the candidates.

Because of the restrictive formats imposed on many of the debates, hastily assembled arguments, as opposed to carefully developed ones, have been reflected in the candidates' oratory. As Jamieson and Birdsell (1988) pointed out, the debates suffer from compression. Time restrictions for candidate responses have been a key element in this problem. The trade-off, of course, in restricting the length of discourse is coverage of an adequate number of topics.

In developing political debate formats, organizers focus on a variety of considerations: speaker time, speaker rotation, the use of opening and closing statements, the use of rebuttals, surrebuttals, and follow-up questions, the restatement of questions, the use of notes by the contenders, the selection of moderator and panelists, and the subject areas to be covered. These considerations also become vitally important to the candidates involved because they impact on their ability to present and defend their own positions, to point out the weaknesses of the arguments advanced by the opponent, and to generate their own agendas. The degree to which candidates can adapt to the constraints of a particular format imposed on them reflects on their ability to perform effectively in the debate context.

THE SELECTION OF DEBATE QUESTIONS

The choice of questions for a political debate is a subject of considerable discussion. Among the concerns are covering national versus regional issues and subjects most current in the campaign versus those of more general scope. Focusing debates on particular limited topic areas has been tested in some debates (e.g., the 1976 Democratic primary forums and a few of the 1984 and 1988 primary debates). Obviously, such restrictions have a direct bearing on the conveyance of issue-related information by candidates. For a campaign keyed to a small number of issues on which the candidates differ, this option seems logical. In the event that the candidates basically agree on issues (such as in a primary campaign), it would seem reasonable to focus a debate on candidate character and abilities. Swerdlow (1984) argued that "Defining debates by topics is desirable because it makes candidates and journalists focus more precisely on specific issues and thus helps the public learn more from each debate" (1984, p. 16).

The problem of asking multiple questions within the guise of a single question has repeatedly appeared, particularly in the context of the general election debates. The candidates face the dilemma of trying to answer each of the independent questions, but none well, or to answer some, but ignore others. Because of imposed time limitations, frequent questions create shorter response times and encourage the press conference format; less frequent questions encourage panelists to hide several questions within a single inquiry.

Jamieson and Birdsell (1988) argued that the present question and answer format does not even lend itself toward substantive debate. At the very least, they believe candidates ought to be allowed to have visual aids. Even though rebuttal opportunities give candidates a chance to respond to their opponents' remarks, a problem arises for the initiator of the original response who is left wide open for criticism; the candidate ends up weighing the benefits of responding to a panelist's question versus opening up new ground to which the opponent will ultimately respond.

Cross-examination by candidates (Oregon-style debating) is a rare feature in presidential debates (e.g., the 1984 and 1988 primary debates). Such a format is, perhaps, appealing from the standpoint that it could be highly informative; however, it might also produce what Alan Schroeder (1989) called a "shooting match" between the candidates and encourage media analysts to look at the event from a winner-loser orientation. Swerdlow (1984) further argued that "People who advocate face-to-face confrontation may be expecting far too much from them. Such confrontations may degenerate into meaningless nit-picking or exchanges of grand accusations that do little to inform voters" (1984, p. 20).

Informal discussion with commentators, another appealing option, has some precedent at the presidential primary level (e.g., the 1968 California Democratic debate between Robert Kennedy and Eugene McCarthy), but is not likely to emerge at the general election level. Polsby argued for this type of debate format, saying that "Skill at this sort of conversation is far more relevant to the conduct of the presidency, because a president must stimulate and participate in this sort of interaction in order to do his job" (1979, p. 185).

THE SELECTION AND ROLE OF DEBATE PANELISTS
AND MODERATOR

The four Kennedy-Nixon debates featured primarily broadcast journalists. Since then, there has been an increasing use of print journalists in mediated debates. A concern about the use of panelists in debates has centered on their objectivity. In the four 1976 presidential primary forums, local experts were utilized as panelists to support the individual topical themes around which each of these events was directed. This option has inherent problems, however; expert panelists tend to advance pet theories and seem to be less polished than their journalistic counterparts because most are not accustomed to appearing on television. In addition, experts may become overly technical in their questioning of the candidates, making it difficult for viewers to comprehend the ensuing dialogue; nor do they offer the visibility of well-known journalists, themselves an audience draw.

Martel (1983) has argued that panelists create a "buffer zone" between candidates. Jamieson and Birdsell (1988) contended that candidates for this reason want panelists. At the same time, candidates are drawn into the dilemma of answering panelists' questions and addressing their opponents. Martel also suggested panelists increase the likelihood that the contenders have to deal with no-win issues. Print media panelists, he has contended, are likely to be more penetrating in their questioning and more substance-oriented; broadcasting panelists, particularly ones who are well-known, tend to be more image-oriented. He has further argued that the more attack-oriented debater would probably prefer to be faced with a print media panelist over a broadcasting journalist.

Some debates have eliminated the use of a panel altogether. For two of the 1980 Republican primary debates and many of the 1984 and 1988 primary debates the proceedings were conducted by a moderator alone. Although a panel may provide control and direction to a political debate, there is a fine line between panelist intervention and facilitation of the candidate dialogue.

One of the least-contested elements of presidential debates is the choice of moderator (Martel, 1983). The traditional moderator role has required the individual involved to more or less orchestrate the proceedings. In the more recent primary debates, in the absence of a panel, the moderator has played a very substantial part by asking the candidates questions, challenging their answers through follow-up questions, as well as legislating the interactive give-and-take of the encounter.

THE ROLE OF AUDIENCE MEMBERS

The use of questions from audience members has been a feature of presidential primary debates but not general election debates. Such questions may be perceived as taking valuable time away from other dialogue. On the other hand, the questions reflect voter involvement in the process and create public presence during the event.

In the 1988 general election debates, the audience role was essentially redefined. Sponsored by the Commission on Presidential Debates, these three debates featured audiences composed of a greater percentage of party representatives as opposed to community representatives, resulting in boisterous audience reactions to candidates' verbalizations.

AGENDA CONTROL

Through content analysis of the 1960 and 1976 presidential debates, Marilyn Jackson-Beeck and Robert Meadow introduced the concept of the triple agenda in political debates, namely the press, the public, and the participating candidates have multiple agendas. The researchers argued that the journalist panelists who ask the questions of the candidates may not ask ones which get at the concerns of the public "for whose benefit the debates are purportedly held" (1979a, p. 179). In turn, the candidates raise new topics in the process of supposedly answering the questions directed to them. Friedenberg pointed out the fact that for the candidates the "motivating exigency" is to be the winner of the election; for the journalist panelists, it is to produce a newsworthy event (1990, p. 207). A problem central to the incorporation of the public agenda in presidential debates, argued Friedenberg, is the fact that no one represents the public interest in negotiation sessions leading to debates.

In their study of the 1960 and 1976 presidential debates, Jackson-Beeck and Meadow found that (1) about one-third of the words emanating from Kennedy, Nixon, and Carter in the debates entailed a direct reply to the panelists or an immediate rebuttal in response to an opponent; (2) 62 percent of the time Ford was responsive in providing direct responses or rebuttals; (3) Nixon, Kennedy, Carter, and Ford addressed 68, 74, 84, and 87 percent of their words, respectively, to self-selected issues. According to Jackson-Beeck and Meadow, "although the candidates would often change the issue or speak on a topic other than that raised by the questioner, they generally stuck to a single issue once they began to speak" (1979a, p. 176).

In a study of the 1976 debates, Lee Becker, David Weaver, Doris Graber, and Maxwell McCombs (1979) noted no significant correlation between the debate agenda and the public agenda of a panel of voters. This finding was confirmed by Steven Brydon who compared the questions raised by panelists with the public agenda, as reflected in public opinion polls. More specifically, he found that the panelists "failed to reflect the general consensus that inflation and unemployment were *the* major policy issues of the election" (1979, p. 331). On the basis of a content analysis of the first 1976 debate, Meadow and Jackson-Beeck concluded, "In 1976 economic concerns were most often named by the public, while the debaters often answered questions in political or governmental terms. In other words, the public could not have heard the candidates addressing issues in proportion to their perceived importance" (1980, p. 55).

In another study of the 1976 debates, Warren Bechtolt, Joseph Hilyard, and Carl Bybee found that the candidates controlled the discussion 44.8 percent of the time in the first debate, 63.7 percent in the second encounter, and only 37.5 percent in their final meeting. On the basis of their analysis, the researchers concluded, "The candidates managed to exercise a measure of control even in the reporter-dominated debate format" (1977, p. 681).

Prentice, Larsen, and Sobnosky performed a content analysis of the 1980 Carter-Reagan debate and found that "the failure of the debate to force the candidates to address the issues was very likely a result of a format which allowed reporters to determine what the issues were." Further, they noted that "when the format became less prescriptive, the candidates not only offered more relevant responses but also began to debate" (1981, p. 13).

A more candidate-controlled interpretation of the debate is provided by Freeman who claimed:

Both candidates did what they had to in order to keep their public role/image intact and attempt to denigrate the other's role/image. They did this by coming to the "debate" with a script of canned, predetermined dialogue that they managed to use, however slight the pretext of its relevance to the question being asked by the panel of newspersons. (1981, p. 23)

More recently, Meadow has advanced the idea of revising the concept of the *triple agenda* to a *sextuple agenda*, arguing that three additional parties have made the agenda control issue more complex. Meadow contends that the six parties participating in the control process are the candidates, the journalists questioning them, the viewing audience at home, the audience in the auditorium, the "spin masters" or political consultants attempting to influence the media interpretation of the event (discussed in length in Chapter 4), and the journalists covering the event.

According to Meadow, an auditorium audience—while present for the 1976 debates—did not become more than an anonymous entity until the 1984 debates when its members interjected laughter and applause into the proceedings and had to be admonished by the moderator to keep quiet. As stated earlier and confirmed by Meadow, in 1988 the greater proportion of party members in the debate audience contributed to more boisterous reactions to the performances of the candidates during the event.

Meadow posited the possibility of even a *septuple agenda* due to an emergent trend he noted in the 1988 presidential campaign. The seventh participant cited by the researcher involves the use of debate footage by both the Dukakis-Bentsen and Bush-Quayle campaigns featuring "audience responses of incredulity, derisive laughter or ridicule—to form the core of a negative spot advertisement" (1989, p. 21).

TELEVISED DEBATES VERSUS TELEVISION DEBATES

Ritter and Hellweg drew a distinction between *televised debates* and *television debates*. Televised debates, they argued, are presented "largely from the perspective of the immediate audience" (1986, p. 8). In this case, an assumption is made that the television camera is covering an event, rather than creating one. The seating configurations for such debates encourage the contenders to address the audience rather than each other, with the candidates typically behind independent podiums (e.g., for the general election debates) or collectively as a panel behind a table (e.g., for a primary debate). These debates are generally characterized by a rigid, formal quality.

Examples of televised debates include the general election debates of 1960, 1976, 1980, 1984, and 1988. Examples of primary debates falling into this category include the 1980 Iowa Republican debate, sponsored by the *Des Moines Register*; the 1980 South Carolina Republican debate, sponsored by the University of South Carolina and the *Columbia Record*; the 1984 Iowa Democratic debate sponsored by Rural America and the Iowa Farm Unity Coalition; the 1984 Iowa Democratic debate sponsored by the *Des Moines Register*; all four 1984 Democratic League of Women Voters debates; the 1988 Democratic "Economics of America" debate, sponsored by the Radio/Television News Directors Association, Iowa

Broadcasting, and KRTA-Radio; the 1988 Democratic "Education '88 Forum" debate, held at the University of North Carolina; the 1988 Republican and Democratic Iowa Democratic debate sponsored by the Brown & Black Coalition; the 1988 Democratic "Presidential Forum on Agriculture and Rural Life," sponsored by the Iowa Farm Unity Coalition, the League of Rural Voters, and the Prairiefire Rural Action organization.

According to Ritter and Hellweg, the television debate is "the undisguised creature of the medium—a political 'talk show' which is created for and by television" (1986, p. 8). In this case, the audience acts like a studio audience for a television program oriented toward talk rather than action (1986, p. 9). The staging for these debates is more inclined to follow that of a talk show, with the candidates sitting in chairs, absent of physical barriers between them such as podiums, presumably to encourage more interaction among the participants. These debates tend to be more free flowing than their televised counterparts, with fewer turn-taking restrictions imposed.

Examples of television debates are only available from primary presidential campaigns. They include the 1980 Illinois Republican debate, sponsored by the League of Women Voters; the 1984 Dartmouth College Democratic debate, sponsored by the House Democratic Caucus and moderated by Ted Koppel and Phil Donahue; the 1984 New York Democratic debate sponsored by CBS and moderated by Dan Rather (interestingly, conducted in the Columbia University Library in a theater-in-the-round configuration, such that the three candidates were obligated to look at one another throughout the debate, rather than the audience); the 1984 California Democratic debate, sponsored by NBC and moderated by Tom Brokaw (broadcast from its Burbank studios); the 1988 "Firing Line" Republican and Democratic debates, moderated by William F. Buckley; and the 1988 NBC debate featuring both the Republican and Democratic candidates and moderated by Tom Brokaw (in the John F. Kennedy Center for the Performing Arts in Washington, D.C.).

Ritter and Hellweg did not take a position as to whether either form of mediated debate is preferable. They did note that different sponsors appear to use audiences variably, thus contributing to one form of debate or the other. For example, print media sponsors tend to be associated with televised debates, using these events as a live public forum they can cover. Broadcast media sponsors tend to be associated with television debates, seeing these encounters as events that they have a part in producing. It is interesting to note that the three primary debates sponsored by television networks in 1984 and 1988 were oriented more toward television debates, while debates during the 1980, 1984, and 1988 primary seasons sponsored by print media organizations tended to be more oriented as televised debates. Ritter and Hellweg further suggested that the television debate is most likely to occur in the early part of a primary season when candidates are more willing to risk an unregulated format structure, as evidenced in the 1984 three-hour Koppel-Donahue debate. They argued that the talk-show format is most workable when there are not many candidates (but more than two), when the debate operates through a single moderator, and "when that moderator competently guides the public discussion" (1986, p. 9).

GENERAL VERSUS PRIMARY ELECTION DEBATES

Primary presidential debates often are more informally structured than general election encounters. Of course, there are definite trade-offs between informal and formal debate formats. The informal format provides the least opportunity for a candidate to hide within the structure of a debate to evade or ignore open discussion of a complex issue. However, the informal debate also provides the least control of the interaction in speaking time and speaking rotation, which tend to be more fluid. Candidates engaged in informal debate have no guarantee that they will have an equal opportunity with their opponents to convey their positions or express counterarguments. A formal structure offers candidates at least the assurance of equal speaking opportunities with their opponents.

The informal option would probably not be a likely choice in a bipartisan encounter because so much is at stake for the candidates. To promote more open, issue-oriented discussion, the formal structure, however, must allow for sufficient rebuttal time and minimal interference by panelists asking the questions.

Michael Pfau (1984) conducted a study of three of the 1984 Democratic primary debates to examine the effects of alternate formats in this context. The three debates analyzed were the Dartmouth College debate sponsored by the House Democratic Caucus (which employed two formats, one in each half), the Columbia University debate sponsored by CBS, and the Pittsburgh debate sponsored by the League of Women Voters. The researcher contended that the specific debates chosen could provide a contrast of four different format approaches. Among his findings were that (1) moderator control is inversely related to the number of candidates participating in the debate encounter; (2) the fairness of the questions posed by the moderator is related to differing formats and procedures, but the focus and clarity of the questions posed by the moderator are not; and (3) the incidence of clash among the candidates and the direction or focus of candidates' responses vary as a function of differing formats and procedures, but the proportion of direct and complete candidate answers to questions and development of support for candidate claims do not.

RECOMMENDATIONS FOR IMPROVED DEBATE FORMATS

A number of recommendations have been made to improve presidential debate formats. McCall (1984) has suggested that (1) follow-up questions be directly related to the initial question, (2) the questions focus on an area of disagreement between the candidates, (3) questions be free of bias, (4) questions reflect a tone of good will rather than hostility, and (5) questions call for explanation and justification of significant policies.

Allowing the moderator to introduce various propositions formulated in advance during the debate itself has been suggested by journalists and scholars (Germond & Witcover, 1979; Kraus, 1964) as a way to improve the debate formats. In this way, the contenders might debate more with one another, with the propositions being the vehicle for initiating interaction, and with the moderator monitoring the interaction, rather than looking to panelists for questions. Martel expressed concern over the use of at least a single stated proposition because candidates might

be wary of placing too much weight on one specific issue, unable to disagree about a proposition of sufficient importance to the electorate to merit attention, fearful that a proposition will favor the opponent—particularly if he is an incumbent more familiar with the issue and with greater research facilities at his disposal—or concerned that such a focus might favor the better debater. (1983, p. 120)

Martel also believes that "for a large percentage of the electorate, the propositional debate might be too complex to follow" (1983, p. 120).

Robert Kemp advocated the strengthening of the role of the moderator and eliminating journalistic panelists altogether, to reduce the potential conflict between "those who write the news and those who make the news" (1987, p. 6).

On the basis of his analysis of the 1980 presidential debates, McCall (1984) suggested it would be useful for the panelists to prepare in a similar fashion to the candidates "by researching what the public's concerns are in the campaign, by identifying key disagreements between the candidates, and by studying the strengths and weaknesses of questioning by previous debate panelists" (1984, p. 104).

In an attempt to reconcile the triple agenda dilemma in debates involving the candidates, the press, and the public, as identified by Marilyn Jackson-Beeck and Robert Meadow (1979a), Jack Kay (1983) advocated format changes. These would enhance the potential for candidate clash and the expression of issue and policy differences between the candidates, allow for follow-up periods for candidates to force each other to address questions, and encourage the use of equal time opportunities for each candidate. In addition, he advocated that more rigorous methods be employed in the selection of debate questions, and admonished reporters who cover political debates to avoid the temptation to instantly analyze what has taken place during debates, instead striving to achieve more balanced coverage.

Michael Pfau (1983) offered four recommendations for future political debates. First, he advocated that the issue agendas employed in debates should emanate from the public and the candidates, arguing that the former has been virtually ignored to this point and that since the press serves as the primary source for the public in the formulation of their agenda, the press would not be left out of consideration. Second, he suggested that questions posed to contenders should be phrased simply and clearly, a practice that he contends will promote candidate clash. Third, he stated that candidates should be provided the debate topics in advance and should be permitted to employ notes and materials in the encounter, arguing that this enhances the ability of the participants to respond in a logical and factual manner. Fourth, he recommends that the role of the press in debate encounters be substantially altered so that debates become engagements between candidates and not between candidates and journalists.

As part of their analysis of the 1976 Carter-Ford debates, Lloyd Bitzer and Theodore Rueter (1980) developed four alternative formats to alleviate the problems associated with panels of questioners and direct examination between candidates. The first, a news interview format, would feature questions posed by an interviewer or panel to both candidates on one or two issues per 60- to 90-minute session, over five or six sessions. The participants would be seated in nonadversarial positions. There would be no time limits on answers, opening and closing statements would be included, but there would be no formal opportunity for rebuttals. The second, a modified Carter-Ford format, would involve the candidates in three or four 90-minute debates, each on a designated topic announced in advance, engaging in structured rounds with the propositions to be covered selected by representatives of the candidates, citizens, and a panel of experts. The candidates would be given opportunities for rebuttals and surrebuttals, and follow-up questions would be employed. One variation of this format developed by Bitzer and Rueter would not feature a panel, another variation would do so.

The third, a modified Lincoln-Douglas format, would require the candidates to engage in debate absent of third-party involvement. If moderators were used, they would simply provide a brief introduction and conclusion, keep time, and offer transitions between presentations. Most likely each debate would feature a single topic, one chosen by the candidates possibly in consultation with an impartial panel. Candidates would provide extended speeches on the subject matter involved and be permitted rebuttal opportunities. The researchers proposed two variations of the extended speech-rebuttal structure: one allowing for rebuttal opportunities and rejoinders after each of the 20-minute extended speech presentations, and then summary statements; the other allowing for opening remarks, then the 20-minute extended speeches, followed by several rebuttal opportunities, and closing summaries.

The fourth, a policy address format, would feature each candidate giving a speech prepared in advance on agreed on issues, perhaps back to back, followed by a series of rebuttal opportunities. The researchers advocate a minimum of four speeches per debate spread out over a one-week period, with four or more such debates over the campaign.

Jamieson and Birdsell proposed an alternative to the current series of general election debates. The first debate would involve only a moderator and the two candidates, eliminating the use of a panel of questioners. The structure of the debate would consist of eight-minute opening statements, followed by six-minute restatement/rebuttal opportunities, and two four-minute elaboration segments. The authors contend that this debate would operate as a "twentieth-century equivalent" of a Lincoln-Douglas debate, such that the moderator would only get involved in the proceedings if the candidates were to wander away from the agreed-on topic, allowing the contenders to engage in direct confrontation.

The second debate proposed by Jamieson and Birdsell would feature a conversational format, one allowing a moderator to introduce questions, focus the discussion between the candidates, and act as an arbitrator as necessary. The format for this debate, they contend, would be modeled after the 1980 Houston primary debate and the 1984 primary debates moderated by Dan Rather and Tom Brokaw.

The third debate contained in the Jamieson and Birdsell proposal would "follow any format on which the two candidates could agree," and should they not be able to come to any such agreement, the format employed in the first debate would be used (1988, p. 200). Jamieson and Birdsell argue for a one-hour nationally televised press conference from each of the two candidates the night after the third debate, with the intent of allowing White House credentialed reporters the opportunity to follow up on any matters unresolved by the debate series. Finally, their proposal speaks to the possibility of each candidate having one hour on election eve to outline "the similarities and differences between the candidates and their visions of the future" (1988, p. 201).

Nelson Polsby has proposed the use of "extended conversations," arguing:

The spontaneous capabilities of a candidate's mind can be discovered far more successfully in conversation, where entitlement to the floor is subject to tacit negotiation, moment by moment, where interruptions are possible, and where all parties to the interaction are responsible for its content, and the straightjacket of question and answer gives way to a more freely flowing discussion. Skill at this sort of conversation is far more relevant to the conduct of the presidency, because a President must stimulate and participate in this sort of interaction in order to do his job. (1979, p. 185)

According to Polsby, this format would feature separate interrogations of each candidate by four interviewers (two selected by the candidate, two selected by the opponent) for an hour.

On the basis of an analysis of the 1988 presidential debates, Prentice (1988) made the following recommendations in regard to general election debates: First, they should involve a narrower range of subject matter than past encounters to allow for more in-depth coverage, allowing "candidates to hold one another more accountable for answering questions either through direct cross-examination or more rebuttal opportunities" (1988, p. 16). Second, the focus on domestic and foreign policy issues in a debate series should be restructured, to avoid repetition from one debate to another. And third, answers to initial questions and rebuttal opportunities should be longer than has been the case in past encounters. As an alternative to present formats, Prentice suggests that follow-up questions emanating from panelists be replaced by cross-examination by the opposing candidate in the following structure: (1) panelist 1 question to candidate A, 45 seconds; (2) candidate A answer, 3 minutes; (3) candidate B cross-examination, 30 seconds; (4) candidate A response, 90 seconds; (5) candidate B rebuttal, 90 seconds; (6) panelist 1 question to candidate B (on the same or a related subject); (7) candidate B answer, 3 minutes; (8) candidate A cross-examination, 30 seconds; (9) candidate B response, 90 seconds; and (10) candidate A response, 90 seconds.

Finally, Prentice (1988) offered the possibility of variable formats within the framework of a single debate, as was the case in the 1980 Carter-Reagan debate, or among the single debate encounters within a general election series.

Kalb (1989) recommended a series of six two-hour presidential general election debates, hosted and sponsored by the three major commercial networks, over consecutive Saturday evenings, the last to be broadcast on the Saturday before the election. He advocated that the last hour and a half of the debate focus on a single public policy issue, foreign or domestic, with the initial half-hour offering a question-and-answer period on a variety of issues. While his proposal suggests that each network would establish the format for its two debates, he assumes that each would assign its principal anchor to the moderator role and would set up a panel of reporters or subject experts. His format would not include a studio audience, nor would it permit candidates to employ visual aids to augment their discourse. He argues that twelve hours of such programming should lower the perceived importance of each single encounter, while at the same time offer the public considerable exposure to the candidates.

Kraus and Dennis Davis contended that changing debate structures, while likely an important concern to scholars and political observers, may not ultimately make a difference for voters. As they put it:

Would an imposed structure force candidates to elevate the public interest above their own private interest in being elected? Would candidates reveal things about themselves and their views on issues which they are otherwise unwilling to reveal? Probably not. Debates must be viewed as part of a larger political campaign system which has many clear deficiencies as well as certain strengths. (1981, p. 28)

Any recommendations for format changes in presidential debates need to incorporate the lessons learned from past debates and evolving agenda control factors in negotiation processes. Meadow has noted:

As debates have become increasingly a part of the political landscape, candidates are recognizing how to use them as part of the overall campaign strategy. From the naive debates of 1960, myth grew concerning the importance of debates. In 1976, the importance of avoiding gaffes was learned, as was the role of the journalists in interpreting events. In 1980, skills of a "great communicator" could be used to charm voters and journalists alike. In 1984, new forms of debate preparation emerged, and the spin doctors gathered to lower expectations and then hype debate performance. And in 1988, the live audience emerged to shill for the candidates and provide audio tracks to be incorporated into political commercials. (1989, pp. 21–22)

Chapter Three

The Verbal Dimension of Presidential Debates

The television and radio stations of the United States and their affiliated stations are proud to provide facilities for a discussion of issues in the current political campaign by the two major candidates for the presidency.
—Howard K. Smith, moderator of the first
Kennedy-Nixon presidential debate
(Kraus, 1977, p. 348)

Thank God it was on television.
—Richard Wirthlin, pollster for Ronald Reagan, after reading
the transcript of the 1980 Reagan-Carter debate
(Jamieson & Birdsell, 1988, p. 218)

Since 1960 televised debates between major candidates for president have represented the only opportunity for the American voters to see the nominees side by side for an extended period of time, during which they are forced to deal with the issues of the day. Yet, presidential debates are television events, featuring both sound and pictures. This chapter focuses on the verbal aspects of the debates. But just exactly what constitutes the verbal component of debates?

First, it encompasses the manifest content of debates. Do the debates primarily involve discussion of the issues of the day, or are they primarily vehicles for the projection of candidate's image? What is the argumentative structure of the debates? What stylistic elements do candidates employ? Second, the verbal component includes the role of the questioners in the debates. Third, it features the political context of debates. What strategies do candidates employ? How do incumbents and challengers differ? These are the principal questions about the content of debates that have received scholarly attention.

GENERAL ELECTION DEBATES

Issues and Images

The concern over whether televised debates emphasize images or issues is a consequence of the medium of television. What the viewers see often overwhelms what they hear. Jamieson stresses that "in the age of television, dramatic, digestive, visual moments are replacing memorable words" (1988, p. x). While debate sponsors often bill these encounters as an informative discussion of the issues, the candidates and the media treat them as television events. To what extent has the verbal content of the presidential debates held since 1960 dealt with issues as opposed to images?

When John F. Kennedy and Richard M. Nixon faced off in their first debate of 1960, tremendous attention focused on the role these debates would play in the electorate's decision. A common research concern has been whether or not the 1960 joint appearances were truly debates or merely vehicles for the projection of images. Charles Siepmann complained that the debates provided "little argument in depth and little explanation of issues in detail" (1977, p. 136). Auer coined the term *counterfeit debates*, claiming that they "emphasized personalities rather than issues" (1977, p. 148). Hallock Hoffman claims that rather than debate the issues, the candidates "sought to impress their viewers by the way they seemed to answer the questions" (Mazo, Moos, Hoffman & Wheeler, 1962, p. 12). John Highlander and Lloyd Watkins claimed, "The 'Great Debates' of 1960 were better television shows than they were well developed and significant discussions of vital issues between candidates" (1962, p. 48) Elihu Katz and Jacob Feldman concluded that the debates "focused more on presentation and personality than on issues" (1977, p. 203). Overall, Dan Hahn summarized the consensus: "There is almost unanimous agreement that the debates do stress personality" (1970, p. 11). On the other hand, Hahn pointed out that "the focus has always been upon image, or upon image as a manifestation of the issues" (1970, p. 14).

Despite the general view that the debates of 1960 were simply personality contests, several empirical analyses of the content of the debates demonstrate a higher level of issue discussion than typical candidate-controlled formats (Ellsworth, 1965; Kelley, 1962; Mortensen,

1968). As Hahn pointed out, "There was more there than personality, if the individual voters had cared to avail themselves of it" (1970, p. 11).

In his doctoral dissertation on the 1960 debates, Jerome Polisky reported candidates dealing with campaign issues with "high clarity" (1965, p. 390). He also found that the candidates lost on the issues thought to be their greatest strengths: "Kennedy lost on the issue of the domestic strength of the United States. . . . Nixon lost on the issue of the status of international prestige of the United States" (1965, p. 379).

Given the apparent contradiction between scholars who claimed the debates were all image and personality and those who maintained that the debates contained significant issue information, how can these views be reconciled? It may be that the issue-image dichotomy is a false one. As James McBath and Walter Fisher put it, "Information relative to the candidate's stand on issues is interpreted as evidence of the kind of man the candidate is in respect to his potential electors, not as proof of his qualifications to hold presidential office *per se*" (1969, p. 18). Kraus and Davis observed that issues and images tended to become linked in the viewers' minds: "Issues were not seen as separate from image, but as one and the same" (1976, p. 59).

Paul Rosenthal's dissertation focused on the impact of ethos in the debates. He concluded that the encounters

were vehicles for the projection of the speakers' personalities and it was the impact of the personalities, the ethos, that created the basic persuasive effect. This type of impact, the evidence suggests, was not related to the candidates' performances as debaters. (1963, pp. 106–7)

However, Rosenthal maintained that "the message of the speech also may be a source of personal response" (1963, p. 40). For example, "The precision and accuracy with which a speaker develops and supports an argument may reveal as much about his character and intelligence as a direct personal reference" (1963, pp. 40–41). Rosenthal concludes that "John F. Kennedy's personality produced the greater persuasive effect in the televised debates" (1963, p. 195).

The overall significance of these studies is that, although viewers were predominately responding to the personal qualities of the candidates, how the debaters dealt with issues may have been a factor in their images. Compared to other modalities of campaign communication, rather than some ideal forensic standard, the 1960 encounters did provide significant issue-related information.

After an absence of sixteen years, 1976 marked the return of presidential debates. The debates again were criticized as shallow and lacking substance. Doris Graber and Young Yun Kim (1978) complained that the debates failed to provide any new information to the public. They acknowledge, however, that for members of their sample interested in the campaign but lacking the time to follow it closely prior to the debates, substantial catch-up learning did occur (1978, p. 412).

Of course, in the wake of Watergate and the pardon of Richard Nixon, one might argue that the most important issue of the 1976 campaign was, in fact, the character of the candidates. Goodwin Berquist argued "that one can say, and in 1976 one should have said, the candidate image is *the* issue in the campaign" (1990, p. 37). Particularly in view of Ford's association with and pardon of Richard Nixon, Berquist found that Carter won the credibility issue in 1976. Berquist concluded: "What the three debates served to do was to create the clear impression among the American public that Governor Carter was at least as qualified as his better-known opponent."

The importance of candidate images as opposed to particular issues was not lost on advisers to the two candidates. Richard Cheney expressed this view of the Ford campaign:

Issues, in and of themselves, were unlikely to have a significant impact on the outcome of the election. But they were felt to be significant in terms of how the candidates dealt with them—that is, they were useful tools for displaying those personal characteristics, or lack thereof, that might qualify a man to be President (1979, p. 115).

Democratic pollster Patrick Caddell shared his Republican counterpart's view of issues as a means to an end: "In the absence of burning issues in a campaign, the voter's perception of a candidate's personality is the most crucial factor in determining a wavering vote" (Lesher, Caddell & Rafshoon, 1979, p. 141).

What images were projected by the candidates in 1976? Bitzer and Rueter claim: "The image projected by Ford was sharply defined and easily understood. He was The President, a fact he underscored time after time" (1980, p. 143). Carter's "image was more complex; in crafting it, he chose to provide multiple definitions of himself" (1980, p. 143). He cited his experiences—from farmer to scientist—in defining himself.

Given these claims, was there any substantive issue content in the debates? According to David O. Sears and Steven H. Chaffee,

The general conclusion that emerges from several content analyses is that the debates themselves were heavily issue-oriented, but the subsequent coverage of them was

decidedly less so. The interrogating reporters spent 92 percent of their time on issues, and the candidates responded with issue-related comments either 77 or 80 percent of the time, depending on the analysis. (1979, p. 228)

Jackson-Beeck and Meadow (1979b) conducted content analyses of the first debates in both 1960 and 1976 and concluded, "In both debates, more than half the issue discussion related to government and over one-fourth dealt with economics" (1979b, p. 334). They trace the rise and fall of other issues over time, finding that defense and foreign policy, health, education, and welfare, were major topics in 1960, but not 1976, while natural resources was an issue in 1976, but not 1960.

William Eadie, Paul Krivonos, and Gary Goodman applied Rosenthal's paradigm to the first 1976 debate. They had expected their subjects to "see the message-related factors (nonpersonal) in a different manner than the source-related factors (personal)" (1977, p. 10). These expectations were not born out. "Instead of being perceived as separate entities, the message items were combined by subjects to again produce the general credibility factors" (1977, p. 10). This study provided empirical support for the previous claims of Caddell and Cheney.

Thus, issues functioned not so much in their own right, but as cues to voters about other matters, such as competence. Ford's 1976 blooper about Eastern Europe was significant for exactly the reason that it reflected negatively on his competence. Ford's press secretary, Ron Nessen stated, "The controversy over the Eastern European gaffe was not about the President's policy. The real damage of the Eastern Europe error was that it revived doubts about Ford's intelligence and competence" (1978, p. 265).

As in 1960, the 1976 debates were not devoid of issue content. However, the issues seemed primarily to contribute to an overall impression of the candidates' images. Especially as buffeted by post-debate commentary (discussed in Chapter 4), Ford's gaffe about Eastern Europe became significant, not because Americans cared about Poland, but because it raised doubts about Ford's competence.

Jimmy Carter, who benefited from the debates in 1976 was to rue them in 1980, when he met Reagan one week before the election. Once again the issue-image question was raised. Berquist and James Golden claimed "The presidential debates were electronic media events in which a speaker's delivery, appearance, and overall manner—as filtered through the television screen—proved to be more important than substance" (1981, p. 132, italics omitted). Auer claimed "The Carter-Reagan debate offered little support for the myth of issue centrality" (1981, p. 19). Reagan, according to Auer,

> was the classic defensive boxer, maintaining his cool and sticking to his basic fight plan. In short, his image was that of a candidate playing the role of a deliberately genial and smoothly competent challenger, adroitly fending off or evading his opponent's grim-faced attacks, and counter-punching just often enough to satisfy his fans. (1981, p. 20)

Martel contended that "Reagan's television personality was so warm and humane that Carter could not make his anti-Reagan charges believable" (1983, p. 49).

Bernard Brock presents a dramatistic analysis of the Carter-Reagan debate. He identifies a positive and negative drama for each man. In the debate, he concludes: "Reagan successfully blunted his [negative] reckless drama and partially re-established Carter's negative drama [that the office of president was too big for him] as dominant" (1981, p. 7).

Despite all of the analysts who credited Reagan's success in the debate to his television personality, as opposed to substance, there are others who argued that Reagan won on substance as well as style (Govang & Ritter, 1981; Riley & Hollihan, 1981; and Ritter & Gibson, 1981). Robert Rowland also challenged the popular view that Reagan won the 1980 debate because his style triumphed over Carter's substance. Rowland concluded:

> Reagan did a much better job of answering specific questions and cited more relevant reasoning and evidence in support of his policies than did Carter. More importantly, Reagan did a far better job than Carter of refuting the charges made against him. (1986, p. 161)

Rowland challenged the view that the 1980 debates were simply contests in image-making. He suggested "Reagan's style and substance defeated Carter in the debate. Such a finding is important because it exonerates the 1980 debate from the charge of being only an exercise in TV image-making" (1986, p. 65).

In fact, journalist Jeff Greenfield agreed that Reagan's success was not due primarily to his television image:

> Of course television communicates personal qualities better than it does abstractions; it is the very essence of the medium. . . . This does *not* mean, however, that Ronald Reagan won the debate on acting ability. . . . If anything, it was Carter who was the media creation, and Reagan who was speaking more naturally, more artlessly, using the arguments he had been using in the political and public arenas for the last three decades. (1982, p. 247)

Greenfield notes that Reagan won the debate, despite Carter's success in placing him on the defensive and despite Carter's skillful weaving of appeals to various constituencies. Greenfield argued "In an ironic rebuttal to the 'substance-doesn't-count' attitude . . . the final tactical battle had been defined by the burden imposed on the incumbent President by his own record" (1982, p. 227).

Again, there is the inherent difficulty of separating issues and images. Robert Weiss addressed this relationship, claiming that "issues and images are in practical fact interlocked and that they intertwine in all manner of convolutions and mutually affect one another in countless ways" (1981, p. 22).

In 1984, Walter Mondale faced Reagan, then a popular incumbent. Despite trailing badly in the polls, Mondale did score an apparent win in the first debate, largely as a result of Reagan's failure to live up to his image as the great communicator. In terms of issue focus, however, the debates were undistinguished. Meadow complained that "debates are not debates by standards of rhetorical and argument analysis" (1987, p. 208). Meadow added: "Debate points are awarded for encapsulation and memorization, not creative thinking" (1987, p. 209). Furthermore, "because of the focus on the blooper, candidates tend to be overly rehearsed, cautious, and uncreative" (1987, p. 209). Debates "are events staged to allow candidates to advertise their campaigns in short speeches" (1987, p. 210).

Drucker and Janice Hunold characterized the encounters as "the Presidential Debating Game" (1987, p. 202). They conclude, "In substance (game strategy), style (use of television features by the director to provide entertainment), and audience perception (as real entertainment), the Debating Game joins a long list of successful televised game shows" (1987, p. 206). In this context, "the emphasis is on the show rather than the game" (1987, p. 206).

Gladys Lang noted the televised nature of the debates has changed the role of viewers from electorate to audience: "Insofar as debates increasingly have been produced with an eye to projecting personal images . . . the viewers are being wooed not so much as an electorate but as an audience" (1987, p. 213). As a consequence, "what matters most to them is not the substance of *what* the candidates say in these debates but *how well* they say it and whether the candidate projects the image he strives to project" (1987, p. 213).

Debates also tend to reduce the differences between candidates. Lang noted that "the rhetoric of televised debates tends to avoid what is dangerously controversial while stressing commonalties that unite all citizens in the pursuit of the common good" (1987, p. 212). Jamieson and Birdsell pointed out that the debates tend to obscure real differences between the candidates, rather than highlight them: "Where actual differences do exist, the debates may not make them clear. . . . [C]andidates stand to gain little and lose much by being specific" (1988, p. 167).

In 1988, for the first time since 1960, a presidential debate occurred without a sitting president. Once again, there was a perception that issues were sacrificed to images. Gary Petty, Kraus, and Tsan-Kuo Chang suggested "that televised presidential debates are in fact perceived by many voters and non-voters as a competitive event in which responses to the debates are similar to responses to sporting events" (1990, p. 24).

Dale Herbeck contended that Dukakis's failure in the 1988 debates resulted from a failure to understand the nature of the encounters. Herbeck claimed Dukakis treated the debates as real debates and thus argued in ways that created a "benevolent technocrat" image (1989, p. 2). Herbeck cited Dukakis's answer to the first question in the second debate (concerning the rape and murder of his wife) as the "best example of the benevolent technocrat strategy" (1989, p. 6). Herbeck claimed, "Presidential debates are more an exercise in image management than debating. By most formal conceptions of debate, Dukakis was a formidable advocate. . . . Yet he lost the battle for public opinion because the viewing audience is more concerned with image than with substance" (1989, p. 12).

Edward Hinck (1989) sees the presidential debates of 1988 as a chance to dramatically enact character. He accepts the premise that in these debates, "character and argument are related" (1989, p. 2). "Thus, in a political debate, an audience deliberates about the qualities of the candidates, not their programs" (1989, p. 4). Because of the focus on character, argument is a means of character enactment, an opportunity to develop a potential president's ethos. Hinck concluded:

Bush was able to project a more coherent vision of leadership and appear more personable than Dukakis. Bush was able to eliminate doubt about his ability to respond spontaneously, genuinely, and coherently to important questions about his candidacy while Dukakis was unable to communicate an equally genuine, personal appeal for his leadership ability (1989, p. 8).

Thus Dukakis was caught in a paradox. While he argued well in traditional terms, "his language choices reinforced an image of a technocratic passionless leader" (1989, p. 13).

Despite the focus on images among critics, there is evidence that at least some viewers were interested in issues. Dan Drew and David

Weaver conducted a telephone survey of 252 respondents in a Midwestern city. They found that despite their limitations, the debates "were useful in making many voters more aware of differences in the issue positions of the candidates" and in "citing issues as more important than candidates' personal qualities in voting decisions" (1990, p. 13). These findings support the view that debates are informative for the electorate.

In terms of the issues, Halford Ryan (1990) analyzed the first debate on each of the major issues addressed. He concluded that "Dukakis heavily discomforted Bush on drugs, the deficit, the abortion issue, the selection of Senator Dan Quayle as a running mate, and on the Iran-Contra affair" (1990, p. 158). Bush may not have won, but he also did not lose. Dukakis reached a level of plausibility as president. In the closing speeches, "Bush reiterated the basic themes of the first and second debates," while "[a]pproximately a third of the governor's short summation was inappropriate" (1990, p. 162). On the whole, Ryan agreed with Charles Wilbanks and William Strickland, "we should not expect great drama. We should not expect an in-depth analysis of the issues, nor should we expect stirring oratory" (Ryan, 1990, p. 162).

Robert Ivie and Ritter pointed out Dukakis's problem in debating foreign policy:

Identifying so closely with Reagan's central theme [peace through strength] created for Dukakis the problem of defining a legitimate campaign issue on matters related to defense and foreign policy. . . . Dukakis resorted to a call for better management of the Reagan agenda, thus creating a kind of rhetorical dissonance between the substance and the spirit of his message. (1988, p. 13)

Dukakis was the "gloom-and-doom" candidate, while Bush was "upbeat" (1988, p. 16). "Thus, the rhetorical flaw in Dukakis's stand on defense and foreign policy was the dissonance between his managerial metaphor and Reagan's heroic vision" (1988, p. 17). On both issues and images, Dukakis was at a severe disadvantage when compared to the vice president.

These studies support the view that presidential debates do contain significant issue content and that some viewers make use of this information. On the whole, however, the televised nature of the encounters encourages a focus on candidate images, with how the candidates handle the issues comprising a means of assessing candidate character. Rather than deliberating about public policy choices, viewers make judgments about presidential character based on the debates.

Argumentation

Given the heavy emphasis on images in the debates, it may be somewhat surprising that a fair amount of scholarship has focused on the argumentation present in the debates. This section looks at the debates as debates. However, one must remember that arguments in television debates tend to be compressed and abbreviated. Jamieson argued that formats allowing only one to two and a half minutes for answers forced "the candidates to capsulize" (1988, p. 10).

The 1960 debates produced several analyses focusing on argumentation. A systematic analysis was conducted by John Ellsworth, who compared the debates with candidates' acceptance and farm speeches. He found that in debates, the candidates *"made clearer statements of their positions and offered more reasoning and evidence to support their positions, than they did in other campaign situations"* (1965, p. 794). He also found that about a quarter of the debate content was in evidential categories. The debates increased Kennedy's use of analysis and Nixon's use of evidence. Ellsworth concluded, "There may be ways in which the debates could be improved; but improved or not, it seems clear that the confrontation of the candidates produced measurable changes in the types of statements they made" (1965, p. 802).

Similar conclusions were reached in other studies. Stanley Kelley, Jr., (1962) found in the debates more acknowledgment of agreement between the candidates than in their speeches as well as more explicit statements of specific programs. The presence of both candidates at one time and the prospect of "imminent rebuttal" helped explain this phenomenon. C. David Mortensen (1968), in a study of candidate-controlled versus network-controlled formats in 1960 and 1964 campaign telecasts, found that "candidates on network-controlled programming are more apt to provide factual substantiation for their policy claims than they are when appearing in traditional campaign situations" (1968, p. 279). He revealed debates to be second only to interview telecasts in candidate support for policy claims. Network-controlled formats (including debates) "showed proportionately greater time devoted to specific policy claims and correspondingly less use of assertion, and more frequent and systematic reliance upon factual evidence and reasoning" (1968, p. 281).

Generally, the consensus opinion was that the argumentation in the 1976 debates was weak. Bitzer and Rueter concluded, "Ford and Carter hardly debated; nor did they adequately answer the questions put to them. Their argumentation was often shallow, often defective in reasoning and evidence, and seldom went beyond the commonplaces uttered from the stump" (1980, p. 4). They found that Carter was more aggressive than Ford and repeatedly pounded him in the second debate. They characterize Ford's performance in the final debate as "submissive" (1980, p. 121). Overall, they conclude that Carter, as a challenger, engaged in extended debate against his opponent, while Ford failed to carry the attack to Carter.

There were some, however, who found substance in the argumentation. One study (Goldhaber, Frye, Porter & Yates, 1977) found that both candidates utilized numerous statistics, examples, authorities, and comparisons as means of supporting their claims. Carter exceeded Ford in supporting his claims in the first and last debate, while both used equal amounts of support in the second round.

Another study (Riley, Hollihan & Cooley) found that in the first debate, Carter was more critical of Ford than the reverse, while Ford was slightly more defensive than Carter. Carter increased his criticism of Ford in the second debate and Ford increased his defensiveness. By the third debate, Carter reduced his criticism of Ford. In the first debate Ford was the greatest user of declarative (unsupported) statements, while the reverse was true in the other two rounds. Furthermore, the amount of statements utilizing evidence declined from 25 percent in 1960 to only 13 percent in 1976. The authors noted Carter's success in bringing out two issues, the economy and leadership. In contrast to 1960, the authors claim "that Kennedy and Nixon more directly answered their opponent's attacks than did Ford or Carter. Thus the 1960 debates were closer to actual debating than the 1976 debates" (1980, p. 18). This is consistent with Steven Brydon's (1979) finding that on only twelve occasions across all three debates did the candidates refute or correct their opponents (six times each for Carter and Ford).

One must consider the quality of argumentation as well as its quantity. Bruce Bryski (1978) asserted "that Ford committed more errors in the presentation of evidence than did Carter. Ironically, Ford used fewer pieces of evidence and made more errors (inaccurate statements) yet was considered the 'winner' of the first debate" (1978, p. 28). Thus, Bryski's research supports Tom Wicker's judgment that the 1976 debates "afforded the two candidates opportunity to make more misrepresentations, false claims, calculated appeals and empty promises than probably ever were offered so directly to a long-suffering electorate" (Jamieson & Birdsell, 1988, p. 190).

The 1980 debates also were studied by argumentation specialists. Ritter and Gibson presented a revisionist position, challenging the view of these forums as "counterfeit debates." Overall, they conclude:

"*Reagan* carried the burden of debating Carter. While media reports of the debates stressed Reagan's affability under fire, an examination of the debate itself suggests that it was Carter who was evading a more direct debate" (1981, p. 7). Donald Govang and Ritter reported on a preliminary content analysis of the 1980 debate and concluded that the 1980 debate, unlike the earlier encounters, "possessed the essential features of a debate" (1981, p. 5).

Ritter and David Henry rejected the conventional wisdom "that Reagan's style triumphed over Carter's substance" (1990, p. 87). Rather, they claimed Reagan's strategy was effective because he "combined sustained argumentation with an appealing style of presentation" (1990, p. 87). Carter, on the other hand, utilized a defective strategy, requiring him "to attack without arguing, to list points without developing them fully, and to hope that Ronald Reagan would defeat himself" (1990, p. 87).

Riley and Hollihan suggested that the 1980 debates were more like the 1960 debates than their immediate predecessors, representing "a return to the direct responses found in the Nixon-Kennedy debates" (1981, p. 58). Thus, the debaters relied more on evidence and analysis than in 1976. Overall, the authors concluded "that the 1980 debates more resembled actual argumentative confrontations than the 1976 debates did" (1981, p. 58). Having debated in two successive elections, "Carter was far more critical of his opponents as a challenger (in 1976) than as an incumbent (in 1980)" (1981, p. 58).

Another study (Tiemens, Hellweg, Kipper & Phillips) reported that Jimmy Carter attacked Reagan twenty-one times, but only refuted him once. Reagan, on the other hand, attacked Carter sixteen times and refuted Carter's attacks fourteen times, a far more even distribution of attack and defense. The authors noted,

Both attacks and refutations made by the two candidates contained considerable use of support and evidence, factual illustration, and historical reference. Emotional appeals were used by Carter about twice as often as Reagan, and were characterized by the use of emotionally laden adjectives. (1985, p. 37)

Thus, Reagan did not avoid confrontation, but refuted Carter frequently, while Carter attacked again and again, but only once refuted Reagan.

The debates in 1984 pitted a popular incumbent president against former Vice President Walter Mondale. There was a marked contrast between the president's argumentation in the two debates. In the first debate, Brydon (1985a) reports that Reagan exceeded Mondale in refutation, but criticized Mondale less than the reverse. Fifteen of

Reagan's twenty-four statements utilized statistics, an untypical reliance on detail for the president. In the second debate the president only refuted his opponent four times and was less critical of Mondale than in the first debate. Mondale was also less critical of Reagan. Notably, Reagan employed only three statistics in the second debate, perhaps in response to criticism of his debating style.

John Morello (1988a) examined the impact of visual structuring on the verbal clash in the 1984 presidential debates. Morello revealed ninety-seven occasions of clash (attacks or refutations) in the two debates. More clash occurred in debate one than two, and Mondale was the greater initiator of clash. However, Morello found that "visual depictions . . . misrepresented these verbal clashes" (1988a, p. 280), a finding discussed further in Chapter 4.

The 1988 Dukakis-Bush debates presented two contrasting styles of argument. Bush was a member of a popular administration and Dukakis faced the challenge of convincing voters that it was time for a change. Ryan noted that while Dukakis risked "advocating change," Bush simply defended the "status quo" (1990, pp. 149–50). Bush emphasized "peace and prosperity, and conservatism," while Dukakis attacked the administration on "drugs and deficit, and tough choices" (1990, p. 150).

Hellweg and Anna Verhoye compared the verbal behavior of Bush and Dukakis in their two debates. They concluded,

Clearly Dukakis was more attack-oriented than his counterpart in both debates. . . . Taking the debates together, Dukakis attacked his opponent in 77 percent of his message opportunities, while Bush did so only 40 percent of the time. Interestingly, Bush engaged in much more refutational commentary in the first debate than in the second debate (29 percent to 9 percent of the messages). (1989, p. 19)

Bush's refutational statements exceeded those of Dukakis in the first debate, but they were equal in the second round. Bush offered more policy statements than Dukakis, who was more negative about Bush than the reverse. Dukakis used more emotional appeals than Bush in the first debate. Bush, on the other hand, used more loaded language than Dukakis. Both candidates employed humor equally. Dukakis was much more likely to directly refer to Bush than the reverse. "Quotable, compelling lines were employed by Bush most often in the first debate (five messages); they were never utilized by his opponent in the second debate" (1989, p. 23). Thus, Bush had a clear advantage going into the sound bite battle after the final encounter.

Carlin argued "that the joint appearances are indeed debates both by definition and in the strategies employed by the candidates" (1989,

p. 208). She claimed "there is no evidence that any presidential debate has been totally devoid of clash and issue presentation" (1989, p. 209). She continued, "An examination of the 1988 debates reveals that even with the format limitations, no cross-examination period, and evasiveness there was direct clash between the candidates" (1989, p. 209). Yet the quality of argumentation in these debates was suspect. For example, Nancy Oft-Rose identified two fallacies in the 1988 presidential debates, "name calling and glittering generalities" (1989, p. 198).

Morello analyzed the verbal and visual aspects of the 1988 debates. Under the verbal domain, Morello reported "99 separate statements of attack and defense" in the debates (1990, p. 4). Dukakis attacked Bush more than the reverse, and more so in the first debate. Yet Bush engaged in more refutation than Dukakis. Overall, "Dukakis expressed 54 utterances of clash (34 in debate one, 20 in debate two) compared to Bush's 45 (29 in debate one, 16 in debate two)" (1990, p. 5). However, visual structuring of the debate "misrepresented the incidence of verbalized clash. . . . [depicting] Bush as the more frequent initiator of clash when Dukakis actually was" (1990, p. 26). He also indicates an emphasis on "*ad hominem* attacks as the verbal cue for the cut to a reaction shot" (1990, p. 26). Finally Bush enjoyed "more opportunities for nonverbal refutation" (1990, p. 26).

Based on these studies, it is clear that these debates can be analyzed from an argumentative perspective. The real question, however, is how the viewer at home responds. Most average voters are probably not trained in judging by standard debate criteria. The studies by Morello (1988a; 1990) point out how the visual dimension of debates can undermine the verbal. In particular, camera shots, cuts, and reaction shots may give the appearance of clash where there is none or even give one candidate an advantage over another. Thus, while scholars can study the transcripts of debates in terms of argument, the viewers at home may well be deprived of a true understanding of the argumentative dimensions of the debates. Chapter 4 explores the visual dimension in more detail.

Style

The style of candidate presentation has been the focus of researchers from the very outset of these debates. Particularly given the general view that debates focus on style more than substance, there has been a desire to identify elements of style contributing to success. Style, may be defined to include linguistic, as well as paralinguistic characteristics of speaking, such as rate and fluency.

The 1960 debates provided an opportunity to analyze the candidates' language use. Larry Samovar (1962, 1965) studied ambiguity and unequivocation in the debates. A key finding was that "people tended to read meanings into a message spoken by a favorable source" (1962, p. 279). Thus, one of the factors leading to selective perception may have been the degree of ambiguity present in candidate statements, which allowed supporters to read meanings into statements that were actually ambiguous. Samovar found that

certain rhetorical characteristics contribute to ambiguity. Such things as weaving rebuttal into your own policy statement, jargon, emotional language, a lack of development, weak or no transitions, unanswered rhetorical questions, and contradictory statements were devices that seemed to be conducive to ambiguity. Techniques such as direct statements, development and explanation, answered rhetorical questions, redundancy, and evidence and support seemed to aid clarity. (1965, p. 218)

Important topics, such as civil rights, farm policy, U.S. prestige, and the dispute over Quemoy and Matsu (islands off the coast of China that were the subject of dispute between Taiwan and China) were discussed in ambiguous passages (1962, p. 279).

The choice of words by the candidates may be indicative of style of presentation. The general impression that Kennedy was more dynamic than Nixon was confirmed by Roger Sherman (1966), who reported that Kennedy's choice of words showed greater dynamism than Nixon's in the first debate.

Jackson-Beeck and Meadow (1979a) compared speaking styles of all four candidates in 1960 and 1976. In 1960, the dominant concern was progress; in 1976, conservation. Kennedy used metaphors of weights and burdens, while Nixon used sports metaphors. Carter used machine metaphors, while Ford, who rarely used images, employed construction images.

Some studies focused on paralinguistic aspects of style, such as rate of speaking and presence of nonfluencies. In the first debate, Jackson-Beeck and Meadow (1979b) found: "As slowly and unimaginatively as Ford spoke . . . his speech was relatively clear and deliberate. Carter, meantime, repeated himself sequentially and otherwise erred, about twice as often" (1979b, p. 337). "Debaters in 1960 were much more fluent than their 1976 counterparts" (1979b, p. 340). Another study (Goldhaber, Frye, Porter & Yates, 1977) reported that Carter employed more nonfluencies than Ford in the first debate. By the second debate, both men were more fluent. In the final debate, Ford was actually less fluent than Carter. Thus, Carter's apparent nervousness in the first round seems to have been less prevalent as the debates continued.

Between the 1976 and the 1980 debates, the significant change Jimmy Carter made in his image was reflected in his language use. Rather than the people's candidate, he was The President. Brydon noted that although Carter in 1976 mentioned "the people" approximately seventy times in three debates, in 1980, Carter referred to "the people" only nine times (1985b, p. 145). He made twenty-seven references to the presidency, as well as ten references to the Oval Office. Ford in 1976 made only about forty references to the presidency and one reference to the Oval Office in the three 1976 debates. Carter engaged in frequent attacks on Reagan, whom he called "dangerous," "disturbing," and "ridiculous." Carter's attempt to appear presidential, while using intense language to launch attacks on Reagan, may have been a source of dissonance in his image.

Of course, Reagan in 1980 proved to be a master of the sound bite. His "There you go again" line became the most remembered feature of the debate with Carter. Four years later, however, that line would come back to haunt him.

In 1984, Reagan's mastery of style came into question. Howard Erlich explained Reagan's loss of the first debate in stylistic terms: "Rhetorical density—Reagan's saturation of the language without enough regard for context and audience—is his central flaw. This results in interjections which confuse and syntax which is confusing" (1985, p. 10). As noted previously, Reagan reduced his use of statistics significantly in the second debate, perhaps seeking a less dense linguistic style.

The 1988 debates were hardly a contest of stylistic giants. Yet there was a difference in the approach of Bush and Dukakis. Ferald Bryan presented a stylistic comparison of the candidates. Analyzing metaphors and style, the author concluded,

Bush was a more artful user of language during these two confrontations. From the first question in the first debate, Bush strongly associated himself with American Values and the popular Ronald Reagan. . . . The narratives referred to by the Vice President were warmly emotional and carefully linked to everyday experience. (1989, p. 18)

On the other hand, "the argumentative style of Michael Dukakis fared poorly on television and especially against the metaphorical perspective that Bush employed" (1989, p. 19). Dukakis "was a fine 'negative' debater, but his vision or plan for the nation was never specifically spelled out for the audience" (1989, p. 19).

Mary-Ann Leon and T. Harrell Allen used computer programs to measure the candidates' language use. The authors concluded that Bush established his credibility by use of more comprehendible language. "He spoke at from two to four grade levels below Dukakis. In general he was less abstract than Dukakis" (1990, p. 22). Dukakis's use of powerful language was tempered with the use of powerless terms and hesitations. "Bush clearly concentrated on the use of ideological terms. Although Dukakis was able to maintain an emphasis on competence in the first debate, he shifted his emphasis to ideology in the second debate" (1990, p. 22). Thus, it appears that Bush's language use was better adapted to the debate context.

As in earlier years, the 1988 debates were dominated by the sound bite. Adrian Frana claimed "Candidates were guilty of ignoring sound arguments, aiming for sound bites from the networks. . . . Sometimes emphasis was placed on symbolism over substance" (1989, p. 201). Thomas McClain agreed: "Sound bites replaced substance and became the building blocks of the campaign" (1989, p. 203).

Television debating style must be understood in the context of the overall campaign. In particular, candidates seek to present well-rehearsed, memorable phrases that will be replayed on the evening news, at the same time maintaining sufficient ambiguity to avoid offending segments of the populace. Language must be kept simple and memorable. As one looks back on the debates of the past three decades, one remembers Kennedy's calls for progress, Ford's Eastern European blooper, Reagan's "There you go again," Mondale's turning of that phrase against him, and Lloyd Bentsen's "You're no Jack Kennedy." Capsulized sound bites have become the essence of debate style in televised debates.

Questions

Although not much scholarly attention was paid to the panelists in 1960, by 1976 researchers began to investigate the nature of the questions asked by the panel, realizing their power to set the agenda and pace of the contest, as discussed in Chapter 2.

Jack Gravlee, James Irvine, and Vancil (1976) viewed the questions asked in 1976 as biased and often trivial. This view is substantiated by Bitzer and Rueter, who indicted the panelists on several points: (1) many questions were not appropriate, contained errors or misinterpretations, or were trivial, irrelevant, or redundant; (2) there were a number of unfocused and unclear questions; and (3) there were adversarial questions

(1980, pp. 75–76). They concluded that "hostile questioning was more often directed to Ford than to Carter; and . . . Carter handled hostility more skillfully than Ford" (1980, p. 127).

Brydon (1979) analyzed the panelists' questions in the Ford-Carter debates and found that panelists emphasized Ford's incumbency and asked more difficult, even hostile questions, particularly in the last two debates. The questions focused on public policy alternatives 86 percent of the time, while 8 percent dealt with personal qualifications and 6 percent with political questions.

McCall evaluated the questions asked of debaters in the two 1980 debates. He found that questioners exceeded their time limits in both debates, particularly in the Anderson-Reagan encounter. Multiple questions and unrelated follow-up questions plagued both debaters. He found the first panel failed to focus on differences between Anderson and Reagan. Both debates were marred by biased questions, although this was most prominent in the first round. The tone of questioning was sometimes hostile in both rounds and frequently did not deal with the most significant issues. Nevertheless, McCall's study "reveals that in the 1980 presidential debates, the second debate panel performed much better than the first debate panel" (1984, p. 104).

Ryan concluded that the second 1988 debate was "disappointing" (1990, p. 159). He criticized the panelists' questions concerning rape and murder, heroes, and likeability as "trite" (1990, p. 160). Michael Weiler criticized the candidates for debating the press, rather than just each other: "Through lengthy declarative prefaces to questions, repetition of questions, hyperbole, and other devices, the press may become as much debater as facilitator of debate" (1989, p. 219). J. Michael Hogan also indicted the role of the press in the 1988 debates: "Not once in the 270 minutes of the 1988 debates did a journalist simply ask a candidate: 'What is your position on such and such an issue?' Instead, each and every question was preceded by a mini-speech—always argumentative and often belligerent" (1989, p. 221). Finally, Hogan complained "The media's trivialization of presidential debates reaches full flower, of course, in the 'instant analyses' which follow each debate" (1989, p. 224). Chapter 4 discusses the media's coverage of these debates in more detail.

Overall, the members of the press who have served as panelists must share some of the responsibility with the candidates for the nature of argument in presidential debates. While the format severely limits issue discussion, trivial, unfocused, and loaded questions further diminish the capability of these debates to discuss the issues of the day.

Strategy and Tactics

As with all campaign events—from the first announcement, through the primaries, conventions, and general election—presidential debates involve strategic and tactical choices. This section reviews the findings of researchers who concentrate on the strategy and tactics of these encounters.

In 1960, of course, there had been no previous experience with televised presidential debates. Some felt that by even agreeing to the debates, Vice President Nixon made a serious strategic error. In any event, both candidates had to develop strategies and tactics that allowed them to address the entire nation while sharing the stage with an opponent and the press.

Windt centered his rhetorical analysis of the 1960 debates around the candidates' strategies for reaching targeted constituencies. Windt identified four strategies utilized by Kennedy: (1) linking domestic and foreign affairs; (2) controlling the domestic issue agenda, while appealing to select constituencies; (3) rebutting Republican charges of "big government"; and (4) calling for "vigorous presidential leadership" (1990, pp. 10–11). Nixon's two strategies were to erase "the 'assassin' image" and refute "Kennedy point by point" (1990, p. 12). Overall, Windt concluded that "Nixon misjudged what people expected from a debate" (1990, p. 15).

At the tactical level, Martel (1983) pointed out the importance of Kennedy's opening statement in the first debate, which communicated "confidence, maturity, and decisiveness" (1983, p. 96). Kennedy stressed that he was not satisfied with the progress being made on the nation's problems, while Nixon responded with a "me too" strategy (1983, p. 96). Jamieson and Birdsell claimed "Nixon chose to engage Kennedy in their first debate, repeatedly summarizing Kennedy's points and addressing his arguments. . . . [T]he vice president won as a debater and lost as a would-be president" (1988, p. 165).

Presidential candidates are, of course, representatives of their respective political parties. Beginning in 1960, Democrats have usually stressed their party identification, while Republicans have sought to broaden their political base. In his dissertation, Polisky found that Kennedy emphasized his own identification with the Democratic party and praised its past leaders, such as Roosevelt. Nixon's strategy was to drive a wedge between Kennedy and the Democratic party. Polisky concluded that "the chief effect of the debates with respect to impact on party identification was that of consolidating Democratic support for Senator Kennedy" (1965, p. 372).

Other researchers support Polisky's view on the importance of party identification. Highlander and Watkins (1962) maintained that Kennedy identified himself with the party of Franklin Roosevelt and "Nixon with the Republicans and the Republicans with a reactionary record" (1962, p. 43). Nixon sought to associate himself with Eisenhower and lower Kennedy's prestige by "attempting to identify Kennedy with Truman" (1962, p. 43). Harvey Wheeler claimed, "The chief issues of the campaign were America's defense posture, her rate of economic growth, her prestige in relation to Russia, and the accidental intrusion of the significance of Quemoy and Matsu. All of these issues were Democratic issues" (Mazo, Moos, Hoffman & Wheeler, 1962, p. 18).

The chief strategy employed between 1960 and 1976 was for the leading candidate to avoid debate with his opponent. However, in 1976, Ford, an unelected incumbent, trailed his little-known opponent, Carter, in the polls. Both candidates believed that they would benefit from debating the other, and so the American public once again witnessed presidential debates.

Each candidate faced a unique challenge in the debates. Carter, although the nominee of the Democratic party, was relatively unknown and inexperienced in Washington politics. Thus, he had to base his appeal on his outsider status. Brydon concluded that "Jimmy Carter, as the challenger in 1976, sought to turn his status as an outsider into an asset, stressing his identification with the American people, promising 'a government as good as our people' " (1985b, p. 139). Carter employed an indirect method of attacking Ford, by identifying him with Richard Nixon and the Republican party. In particular, he typically referred to the "Nixon-Ford" administration (1985b, p. 342). Ford, on the other hand was an unelected incumbent, who had pardoned his predecessor. Ford, of course, emphasized "his status as president" (1985b, p. 141). Carl Kell (1976) concluded that the second debate between Carter and Ford was a confrontation of Ford's "rhetoric of the Oval Office" versus Carter's identification with the "fireside chat."

Martel noted that while Carter attacked Ford on the economy, Ford tried to make Carter take specific issue stands. Carter, on the other hand, protected his broad-based support by avoiding specific positions on foreign policy. His pollster, Pat Caddell, advised Carter to please both conservatives and liberals: "Hit him [Ford] from the left and from the right" (Martel, 1983, p. 103). Bitzer and Rueter concluded that the record of the incumbent Ford was a "large target" for the panel as well as Carter.

Ford "was punched and forced to defend, then driven to a new topic without time to conceive a strategy. Relatively unprepared with common-places and unskilled in rapid verbal combat, Ford lost" (1980, p. 144).

In 1980, the situation was complicated by a third major candidate, John Anderson, who was supported by 15 to 20 percent of the electorate, according to polls (Trent & Friedenberg, 1983, p. 248). Carter declined a three-way debate, despite the invitation extended to Anderson by the League of Women Voters, based on his standing in the polls. After a two-way debate with Reagan, Anderson began to tumble in the polls. By mid-October, the League of Women Voters determined that Anderson was no longer eligible to debate, and they issued an invitation to Carter and Reagan to debate jointly (Trent & Friedenberg, 1983, p. 250). Martel (1983, pp. 16–18) reports that Reagan's advisers were divided on whether or not he should debate. The candidate himself made the decision to debate Carter one-on-one, according to Martel. Carter, who earlier had sought a one-on-one debate with Reagan, had been closing in the polls, and hoped to avoid a debate. Ritter and Henry (1990, pp. 72–73) reported that on October 14, Carter's campaign considered giving Reagan an ultimatum for a debate by the end of the week, which the president's advisers knew would sabotage the possibility of a debate. However, Carter was forced to debate when the League of Women Voters dropped its insistence on Anderson's participation and Reagan accepted the invitation. Thus, one week before the election, Carter and Reagan met face-to-face.

Serving as one of Reagan's debate advisers, Martel provided valuable insight into the governor's strategy: Reagan targeted "Republicans and ticket splitters." Rather than attack Carter, Reagan sought to remain "presidential." He "was advised not to surpass, but to respond in kind to the tone and amount of attack leveled by Carter" (1981, p. 41). Martel calls Reagan's "There you go again" line "a masterstroke" (1981, p. 44). Martel also credits Reagan's "five rhetorical questions" from his final statement as equal or better than the "There you go again" line. Overall, Martel concluded "that Reagan outperformed Carter, that he succeeded in making Carter's record the issue of the debate, [and that he] defused the 'mad bomber' image" (1981, p. 45).

Carter's strategy was to make Reagan the issue in the debate. Samuel Popkin sent a memorandum to Carter's pollster, Caddell: "We want a vote between two futures, not a vote of approval or disapproval on the last four years" (Martel, 1983, p. 20). Because Carter's own image was not susceptible to much manipulation, he focused on defining his opponent's image, which was less solid. Martel noted that Carter controlled the issues of the debate, keeping Reagan defensive. Yet, Reagan "maintained his genial personality throughout, and deflected Carter's attack with a combination of humor and righteous indignation" as exemplified by "There you go again" (1983, p. 25).

Brydon concluded that Carter faced a dilemma in 1980: "The Carter strategy required that Reagan make mistakes, as Ford had done in 1976. Without these, Carter would be forced to try to attack and appear presidential at the same time" (1985b, p. 144). "Carter's approach was virtually a mirror image of the rhetoric that earned him the presidency. In 1976, Carter prided himself on being an outsider, but in 1980, he stressed his image as the president" (1985b, pp. 144–145). Yet, that very presidential image was basically incompatible with the attack tone he took in the debate.

In 1980 both candidates had some similar goals. Ritter and Henry identified four goals common to both campaigns: (1) managing pre-debate expectations to their candidate's advantage, (2) appealing to targeted voter blocs, (3) focusing on their opponent's weaknesses, and (4) stressing their candidate's strengths (1990, p. 74). According to Ritter and Henry, "Carter employed a 'hit and run' style of debate" (1990, p. 81). Because Carter "tried to squeeze every theme and every target audience and every issue into his debate speeches," there was very little opportunity to respond to Reagan's charges (1990, p. 83).

Presidential debates had become virtually institutionalized by 1984, as evidenced by Reagan who, despite his impressive lead in the polls, consented to two debates with Mondale. Each candidate had very different goals in the debates. Craig Allen Smith and Kathy Smith found that Reagan had the following goals in order of importance: holding on to his support, going after swing voters, and softening Mondale's support. Mondale, on the other hand, had a far more difficult goal, to convince Americans not to reelect their popular president. To achieve this goal, he needed to "create dissonance about the Reagan presidency by showing that Reagan and his record were not what people thought them to be" (1990, p. 99). Mondale also needed to bolster his image while undermining Reagan's. This placed the challenger in a difficult dilemma. Mondale had to attack Reagan without creating a backlash that would heighten the president's public support. If he failed to attack, there would be no basis for rejecting Reagan.

In the first debate, Smith and Smith found that Mondale employed an "indirect strategy" (1990, p. 101). He also mastered Reagan's own strategy of one-liners when he turned the president's "There you go again" line against him. However, as they pointed out, "By using one-liners to advance a cluster of otherwise tenuous arguments, Mondale overshadowed his clearly reasoned answers. . . . The era of one-liners had arrived" (1990, p. 102). They characterized Reagan's performance in the first debate of 1984 as "perhaps the least impressive moment of Ronald Reagan's illustrious rhetorical career" (1990, p. 103). They pointed out that Reagan, in his desire to reach Democratic voters, relied on "Democratic rather than Republican themes" (1990, p. 105). They also noted that his poor delivery raised the spectre of his age as an issue in the campaign. Finally, Reagan suffered from inflated pre-debate expectations in comparison to Mondale.

Smith and Smith found several improvements in Reagan's debating in the second debate. His "theme was that he was fully in command of a strengthened America" (1990, p. 109). He stressed this theme by using personal pronouns, asserting personal responsibility, utilizing humor, and finally using indignation. Of course, Reagan's response to the age issue became the best remembered sound bite of the debate: "I want you to know that I also will not make age an issue of this campaign. I am not going to exploit, for political purposes, my opponent's youth and inexperience" (1990, p. 110). In the second debate, Mondale tried to stress the theme of being "tough and smart" (1990, p. 112). Mondale, however, jeopardized the positive image he had gained in the first debate by engaging in attack. Finally, the debate ended up focusing on Reagan's accomplishments, thus "affirming Reagan's control" (1990, p. 113). They concluded, "Faced with inflated expectations . . . Mondale did well, but not well enough. Reagan improved sufficiently to confound Mondale's efforts to portray him as incompetent" (1990, p. 115).

Kay rejected traditional argumentation as an approach to studying the 1984 debates. Adopting Walter Fisher's narrative paradigm, Kay contended: "It makes a great deal of sense to believe that the American public responds and understands political debates not as a collection of facts to be verified but rather as a forum in which candidates present competing stories" (1984, p. 10). Utilizing focus groups, he studied the use of "narrative probability (what constitutes a coherent story?), narrative fidelity (do the stories ring true with what people know to be true in their lives?), and good reasons (what standards do people use to judge stories?)" (1984, pp. 10–11). His preliminary findings show that untrained subjects' reactions are better explained by narrative rather than traditional argumentative criteria and that their discussion of the debates involved more frequent use of narrative criteria (1984, pp. 12–13).

The 1988 debates provided both candidates the opportunity to improve on images which had been somewhat tarnished by a divisive campaign that focused more on Willie Horton, saluting the flag, and riding in tanks, than on substance. Ryan claimed, "The successful debater may be more realistically conceived rhetorically as one who shares, more than shapes, the common concerns of the time" (1990, p. 145). According to Ryan, "Bush won the 1988 election because his rhetoric was more reflexive than Governor Michael Dukakis's" (1990, p. 145). Employing a narrative perspective, Brydon reached a similar conclusion: "Bush better fit his narratives to the beliefs of the audience, who were largely satisfied with the Reagan legacy. Bush also demonstrated consistency with President Reagan's narratives" (1990a, p. 24).

In terms of debate strategy, Ryan observed that Bush's goals were essentially to avoid mistakes. His strategy demanded a comparison of values between himself and Dukakis. "Thus, Bush would spend as much time in defining what he was not, which was Dukakis, as in defining what he was" (1990, p. 149). Dukakis, whose image Bush tried to define, sought to define himself and discomfort the vice president. According to Ryan, Bush emphasized "peace and prosperity, and conservatism," while Dukakis attacked the administration on "drugs and deficit, and tough choices" (1990, p. 150).

Each election has forced candidates to develop strategies for their own particular needs. Kennedy and Carter needed to overcome doubts about their experience. Nixon needed to erase his "assassin image" and Ford needed to establish his legitimacy as president, having inherited the job from Nixon. Reagan needed to defuse the "mad bomber" image, while Carter took refuge in his ownership of the Oval Office. Mondale tried to disassociate a popular president from his policies, while Reagan sought to assure America he was not too old to be president. Dukakis tried to overcome the "passionless technocrat" image, while Bush wrapped himself in the flag and identified with Reagan. It is difficult to generalize about strategies, simply because they are so context bound. One particular strategic context, however, deserves further attention, because it involves three out of five sets of debates. The next section reviews incumbent and challenger strategies in televised debates.

Incumbent and Challenger Strategies

A special subset of debate strategies concerns incumbent presidents and their challengers. Three sets of debates—1976, 1980, and 1984—involved incumbent presidents. In addition, 1960 and 1988 involved sitting vice presidents, who shared at least perceived responsibility for the successes and failures of their respective administrations.

In 1960, as the challenger, Kennedy focused on an "I'm not satisfied" strategy, implying that he could do better than the incumbent administration, while Nixon employed a "me too" strategy (Martel, 1983). However, on one particular issue, Nixon faced a dilemma as the incumbent vice president who had access to classified information. In the final debate Kennedy called for the overthrow of Fidel Castro in Cuba. Nixon knew, of course, that the Eisenhower administration had plans to do exactly that. He responded with "a deliberate lie intended to cover up the CIA training of Cuban exiles that was already underway. . . . Nixon declared publicly his opposition to a policy that he vigorously supported in private" (Windt, 1990, p. 23). Thus, the 1960 presidential debates raised the sticky issue of whether or not a member of the incumbent administration should risk national security or deliberately lie when confronted by the possible revelation of government secrets.

Although there was no incumbent president in the 1960 debates, the issue of whether a sitting president should debate was raised in post-debate discussion. Kelley prophesied:

An incumbent is necessarily identified with a record, and a record necessarily involves having made decisions on concrete and controversial issues. A challenger, pointing to past errors and promising to do better, can hope to exploit dissatisfaction with the record in groups of quite diverse interests, provided he does not go into too much detail about changes he would make. An incumbent who used the debate situation to challenge the challenger, forcing him to get down to specifics could greatly lessen the efficacy of this strategy. (1962, p. 361)

In 1964 Lyndon Johnson avoided debate with his challenger, as did Nixon in 1972. Thus, Kelley's predictions remained untested for sixteen years.

In 1976 Ford, trailing in the polls, was eager to debate his Democratic opponent, Carter. After sixteen years without presidential debates, these encounters provided a test of whether or not an incumbent president could successfully debate his challenger. Both Carter and Ford adopted strategies based on their respective status as either challenger or incumbent. As Kelley (1962) had predicted, Carter took the opportunity to blame the incumbent for the ills of the nation, while Ford wrapped himself in the mantle of the presidency and sought to force his challenger to take specific issue positions (Brydon, 1985b).

In 1980, Carter had to defend his policies against the challenger Reagan, who asked the American people if they were better off than they had been four years earlier. Carter, who had been the people's candidate in 1976, became tied to the Oval Office in 1980 (Brydon, 1985b).

Ritter and Hellweg surveyed the research on the 1976 and 1980 debates and identified what they termed *the incumbency factor*. They cited three basic characteristics of incumbent debating: "(1) failure to pursue extended debate, (2) a declarative style of arguing, and (3) a focus upon the status quo rather than a vision of the future" (1984, p. 3).

Prior to 1984 the conventional wisdom had been clear: "*Debates are the vehicles of challengers*" (Caddell, cited in Drew, 1981, p. 411). The 1984 debates refuted that truism. Brydon (1985a) analyzed Reagan's debating in terms of the incumbency factor hypothesized by Ritter and Hellweg (1984). He concluded that the incumbency factor was not a good predictor of Reagan's debate style. In the first debate, Reagan actually debated and supported his arguments, particularly with statistics. In the second debate, the president employed a more declarative style, typical of incumbents. However, he stressed his vision of the future, emphasizing "value images" (DeStephen, 1981), departing from the typical incumbent debate style.

In 1988, Bush, although not the incumbent president, was the vice president, and he tied his campaign to the success of the Reagan years. In fact, at one point, he offered to take all of the blame for the Reagan failures if he could share just half the credit. Bush's ties to the incumbent administration were an asset, not a liability, given the popularity of Reagan.

Thus, one may conclude that the failure of incumbents to succeed in presidential debates in 1976 and 1980 is explained not because of any inherent flaw in their debating style, but because they had difficulty in defending the status quo or in showing that they would change it. In one sense, every presidential debate since 1960 has turned on the question, "Are you better off today than you were four years ago?"

VICE-PRESIDENTIAL DEBATES

1976

On October 15, 1976, for the first time in history two candidates for vice president faced each other and the American people on television. The Mondale-Dole contest drew a 20 percent smaller audience than the presidential contests (Vatz, Weinberg, Rabin & Shipman, 1976). Yet, the importance of the encounter was reinforced when the moderator noted that three of the past five vice presidents had succeeded to the White House. Even though this debate did not draw the same scholarly attention as did the presidential debates, three rhetorical analyses were conducted and are reviewed next.

Bitzer and Rueter (1980) included the vice-presidential debate in their analysis and conclude that tone rather than issues was most important: "Mondale debated ably and with dignity. . . . Dole joked, often inappropriately; he used ridicule and personal abuse; his attitude toward the debate and his opponent seemed flippant; and he made numerous substantive claims that defied logic and history" (1980, pp. 35–36).

Another study (Vatz, Weinberg, Rabin, & Shipman) applied Rosenthal's theories to the Mondale-Dole vice-presidential debate. Dole lost the encounter partly because of his "acid-like" comments. Overall, they concluded that the debate probably exemplified "Rosenthal's 'personal communication.' Vice-Presidents' views are probably not seen in terms of their substance so much as in terms of whether, upon the unlikely (*perceptually, not statistically*) assumption of the Presidency, we will not have a totally inadequate President" (1976, p. 22).

Kevin Sauter believed that Dole faced a much more difficult task than Mondale. While Mondale could remain above the fray, Dole had to gain support from Reagan followers and woo Independents. Furthermore, he had to defend an administration he had criticized. Dole lost the debate as he attempted to implement his strategies. "In addition, his personal style as a slashing campaigner led to the use of humor as an ill-advised tactic to belittle the Democratic ticket" (1990, p. 60). Sauter believes that Mondale, on the other hand, had strategic goals compatible with maintaining his presidential image. He attacked Ford and praised Carter, reinforced his party's themes, and kept his delivery restrained and presidential. A key to the outcome may have been that while "Dole was witty and sarcastic, Mondale was low-key and sincere" (1990, p. 60).

Finally, the vice-presidential debate may have had a long-term impact on Dole's political career. Sauter contends that Dole made "what might be considered the biggest mistake of his political career" (1990, p. 45). By blaming the Democrats for World Wars I and II, as well as Korea and Vietnam, Dole opened up the opportunity for Mondale to respond, "I think Senator Dole has richly earned his reputation as a hatchet man tonight" (1990, p. 46). As Dole himself later acknowledged: "I went for the jugular all right—my own" (1990, p. 65).

1984

On October 11, 1984, Geraldine Ferraro became the first female nominee for national office to debate her opponent on television before the American people. This historical encounter has been the subject of several rhetorical studies.

Patricia Sullivan (1989) examined the Bush-Ferraro debate in terms of differences in male and female communication patterns. Sullivan contends that Bush used masculine terms, especially sports and war metaphors, to raise "questions about the legitimacy of Ferraro's participation in the event" (1989, p. 330). Bush also addressed his opponent as "Mrs. or Miss Ferraro, rather than Congresswoman Ferraro, a form of address agreed upon prior to the debate" (1989, p. 336). Ironically, as Sullivan points out, "she is not really Mrs. Ferraro; she is Mrs. Zaccaro" (1989, p. 336). This strategy was continued with Bush's post-debate comment, "We tried to kick a little ass last night," a statement he excused as an "old Texas football expression" (1989, p. 335). Sullivan contended that Ferraro refused to play the game proposed by Bush. Rather than dull or subdued, Sullivan suggested that "Ferraro might be viewed as the heroic figure who broke frame and refused to participate in Bush's competitive stories" (1989, p. 340).

Dayle Hardy-Short provided an insider's view of Ferraro's preparation for her debate. She reported that Ferraro's staffers had anticipated every question asked in the debate. The pre-debate tactics of Bush's campaign placed Ferraro in a difficult position. For example, Barbara Bush referred to Ferraro as "that four million dollar—I can't say it, but it rhymes with rich." Peter Teeley, Bush's press secretary, told a reporter that Ferraro was "too bitchy" (1985, p. 14). Clearly, the Bush strategy was to place his opponent in the difficult position of being either bitchy or subdued. Thus, Hardy-Short reports that "Ferraro made the decision to tone down her delivery and to deal with issues rather than innuendos" (1985, p. 16). Hardy-Short also blames the format for a lack of confrontation in the debate. For example, Ferraro's response to a panelist, "[A]re you saying that I would have to have fought in the war in order to love peace?" (1985, p. 19) was planned for Bush, not a panelist. The author concluded that "the format was probably as responsible for Ferraro's 'subdued' manner as anything else" (1985, p. 19).

Hinck viewed the debate in terms of "dramatic enactment of leadership" (1990, p. 3). He identified two roles for vice-presidential candidates: "advocate for the presidential ticket and advocate defending their own qualifications for office" (1990, p. 30). He concluded that "both candidates can be judged successful" (1990, p. 20). Bush defended the Republican ticket and Ferraro established her credibility as a candidate for national office.

Hellweg and Drew Kugler conducted a rhetorical analysis of the debate. They found "that Bush employed more direct statements of policy, provided development and explanations more frequently, used support and evidence more frequently, and employed more loaded language than his counterpart" (1985, p. 12). Among his faults were use of "unfamiliar jargon and ineffective transitions" (1985, p. 12). The vice president "relied more often on analogies, historical references, and factual illustrations than Ferraro" (1985, pp. 12–13). "Ferraro utilized the 'shotgun blast' technique and attacked her opponent more frequently than did Bush, basically in the tradition of a challenger role in a debate" (1985, p. 13). Finally, both candidates focused on their opponent's ticket and issued emotional appeals, historical references, and factual illustrations.

Judith Trent attributed the perception of Bush as the winner of the debate to his "overwhelmingly successful merger of incumbency and challenger rhetorical styles" (1990, p. 128). On the other hand, he suffered from an exchange with Ferraro, which conveyed a patronizing attitude toward her and which received much post-debate media coverage. On the issue of terrorism in Iran and Lebanon, Bush said, "Let me help you with the difference, Mrs. Ferraro, between Iran and Lebanon" (1990, p. 132). This comment elicited Ferarro's most memorable response. "I almost resent, Vice President Bush, your patronizing attitude that you have to teach me about foreign policy" (1990, p. 132). After the debate, Bush made his "kick a little ass" statement. As Ann Lewis put it, Bush revealed "a contempt for women that had been implicit in their policy and is explicit in their rhetoric" (1990, p. 134). Trent also identified some problems with Ferraro's style of debating: "She frequently used hedges such as 'let me say' or 'I think' and disclaimers such as 'let me put it this way' or 'from another perspective'—two elements that contribute to powerless speech" (1990, p. 138). Thus, her powerless style of speaking undermined her efforts to portray herself as experienced and competent. Trent concluded, "Although the polls gave Bush the victory, Ferraro was generally perceived as having done very well" (1990, p. 140).

1988

In 1988, the Republican nominee for vice president was probably the most controversial since George McGovern's choice of Thomas Eagleton. Thus, when Lloyd Bentsen and Dan Quayle met on October 5 in

Omaha, Nebraska, considerable media attention focused on the presidential understudies.

Warren Decker reported that Quayle focused his attack on Dukakis, rather than his counterpart, while Bentsen focused his fire on Quayle's competence and, by inference, Bush's judgment. Decker criticized the debate for lacking argumentative clash, support for assertions, or direct answers to questions. Decker claimed that Bentsen provided more detail in his answers than did Quayle. In their use of language, Decker concluded that both candidates mangled their statements, but that overall, "Bentsen's selection of language was much better during most of the debate" (1990, p. 177). Decker also reported that Bentsen utilized "a veiled fear appeal," in contrast to Quayle, who "wanted the viewers to 'feel good' about themselves" (1990, p. 177). Decker credited both candidates with using humor successfully.

The most remembered feature of the debate had nothing to do with the statistics, analysis, or evidence. After Quayle compared himself to another young senator seeking national office, Bentsen replied: "Senator, I served with Jack Kennedy, [pause] I knew Jack Kennedy, [pause] Jack Kennedy was a friend of mine. [pause] Senator, you are no Jack Kennedy" (1990, p. 179). As with presidential encounters, the vice-presidential debates are geared toward sound bites and spin control. An analysis of post-debate coverage (Brydon, 1989) reported that the "no Jack Kennedy" clip received prominent coverage on all three major networks.

Despite an overwhelming perception that Quayle was defeated by Bentsen, the vice-presidential debate appeared to make little difference in the final outcome. It may be that the post-debate commentary had a "dampening effect" (Ferguson, Hollander & Melwani, 1989). A survey of students from four geographical areas found that "vice-presidential debates are even less significant in terms of impact" than presidential debates (Payne, Golden, Marlier & Ratzan, 1989, p. 434).

Comparison of Debates

Are there any commonalties across these three vice-presidential debates? Hellweg and Matthew Stevens compared argumentation strategies in all three debates. They concluded that despite differences, there were some commonalties: "Although the number of attacks directed at the top and the bottom of the tickets varied across the races, the total number of attacks and negative references directed toward the two levels was relatively even" (1990, p. 54). However, the authors indicate that the vice-presidential nominees were more interested in attacking the other ticket, rather than praising the man at the top of their ticket. Hellweg and Stevens also indicated that vice-presidential nominees, particularly incumbents, used "uniting terminology such as 'we' and . . . statements that they agreed with their running mates" (1990, p. 55). With the exception of Bush's references to Ferraro, the candidates employed titles in addressing their opponents. This finding reinforces the likelihood that Bush's strategy in addressing Ferraro was an intentional strategy.

Thus, although subject to less research than the main events, the battles between candidates for the number two job have provided interesting insights. Just as presidential debates are usually remembered for their sound bites, the three vice-presidential debates tend to be remembered for their most dramatic moments. Dole's inexplicable blaming of the Democrats for all of the century's wars, Ferraro's indignant response to Bush's patronizing attitude, and Bentsen's "no Jack Kennedy" retort will probably be recalled long after the specific arguments of these debates have faded in the nation's collective memory.

PRIMARY DEBATES

Thus far, this chapter has focused on the interparty debates held in the general election. However, primary election debates have become an increasingly prevalent feature of the presidential nomination process. This section reviews the findings of researchers regarding the verbal content of these intraparty forums.

Although not the first televised primary debate, the Kennedy-Humphrey debate in West Virginia in May 4, 1960, was the first intraparty debate to receive attention from communication scholars. Berquist examined the rhetorical strategies of the two candidates. While Hubert Humphrey presented himself as a partisan leader, Kennedy projected himself as a "leader of all the people" (1960, p. 2). Kennedy utilized statistics as his most frequent form of support, while Humphrey failed to support many of his assertions. Kennedy used a "common" style of speaking, while Humphrey was a "platform orator" (1960, p. 3), a style ill-suited to the intimacy of television. Kennedy's "presidential-oriented" image contributed to his defeat of Humphrey, who was "candidate-oriented" (1960, p. 2). Voters were apparently more interested in a potential president than a political partisan, even in a primary election.

Hermann Stelzner (1971) utilized the courtship principle to analyze Kennedy and Humphrey's rhetoric. Humphrey failed to court West Virginia voters because his statements "indicate that he is interested first in the Presidency and the Democratic Party, second, in keeping Richard

Nixon and the Republicans from the Presidency, and third, in West Virginia" (1971, p. 26). On the other hand, "Kennedy has a better grasp of his objectives and better controls and implements his rhetorical choices" (1971, p. 28). Thus Kennedy engaged in "successful political courtship of West Virginia" (1971, p. 33). Humphrey failed to adapt to the localized nature of a primary election debate.

The next primary debates to receive significant scholarly attention were the 1980 debates among the Republican contenders. One study (Blankenship, Fine & Davis) presented an insightful rhetorical analysis of how Ronald Reagan emerged from the primary debates as the party nominee. Utilizing the theories of Kenneth Burke, this study argued that Reagan was transformed from actor to scene. Thus he moved to the foreground of media attention in the debates:

Reagan himself, the other candidates, the press, and the moderators in the debates helped Reagan establish his presence through a series of frames before, during, and after the debates. These frames placed Reagan in the foreground of attention; as he came to dominate more and more frames he became the scene. (1983, p. 28)

The debates allowed Reagan to deliver "well-rehearsed lines" that reflected his basic campaign themes (1983, p. 33). He was able to "envelop [contain] the themes of the other candidates" (1983, p. 33) and ultimately emerged with the Republican nomination and the presidency.

Blankenship and Marlene Fine (1984) studied the Illinois primary on March 13, 1980. Republican hopefuls turned their fire on John Anderson, effectively isolating him from the mainstream of the Republican party. The authors concluded that his exorcism from the Republican party legitimated his candidacy: "Clearly, in attempting to isolate John Anderson, his GOP rivals had 'named' him as someone to be reckoned with" (1984, p. 25). This debate demonstrated that even in losing a primary encounter, a candidate may be legitimated for subsequent elections, even the general election, in the case of Anderson.

The Houston debate between Reagan and Bush took place on April 23, 1980. Hellweg and Steven Phillips (1981b) conducted a verbal and visual analysis of the debate. In the verbal domain, they found the strongest difference between the candidates was in their speaking styles: "While Reagan relied heavily on a conversational speaking style . . . Bush relied heavily on a dynamic speaking style" (1981b, p. 32). Both candidates focused on Jimmy Carter in their attacks, rather than one another. Major differences between the candidates included (1) Bush's greater use of unfamiliar jargon, (2) Reagan's less effective use of transitions, (3) Bush's greater use of emotional appeals, (4) Reagan's greater use of humor, (5) Bush's greater use of hypothetical illustrations and historical instances, (6) Bush's greater use (adequately and inadequately) of development and explanation, and (7) Bush's greater use of restatement at the conclusion of messages (1981b, p. 38).

Harriet Briscoe Harral (1984) compared New Hampshire primary debating in 1980 and 1984. She claimed that the violation of ritual expectations was the most likely correlate of press attention to the debates. For example, in 1980, the first debate, which involved all of the Republican candidates, received scant attention. Yet *The Nashua Telegraph* debate was highlighted by a controversy over whether or not it would be limited to Reagan and Bush. Reagan's line, "I am paying for this mike, Mr. Breen" (1984, p. 7), was widely replayed on television, even though the original debate was not televised. Harral attributes the increased coverage to the violation of ritual expectations. Similarly, in 1984, it was the debate moderated by Ted Koppel and Phil Donahue that received greatest media attention because of its wide-open format. Harral claimed, "The new format, the 'star' of the debate, was largely dictated by the need to make politics engaging on television" (1984, p. 5). "Charges from Glenn of 'vague gobbledygook' and countercharges from Mondale of 'voodoo numbers' and 'baloney' heated the air" (1984, p. 9). A second debate in 1984, held at St. Anselm's College, was traditional in format and largely ignored by the media. Thus, Harral concluded that "the content of the New Hampshire debates counted for little in the overall campaign. The ceremonial aspects of the debates, however, counted heavily" (1984, p. 10).

In discussing the problems with primary debates, Scott Deatherage (1990) noted that (1) format constraints are more complicated due to the larger number of candidates, (2) candidates are forced to resort to gimmicks to stand out from a crowded field, and (3) few voters attend to these debates. All of the factors accentuate the sound-bite approach to primary debating. Thus, from 1988, we tend to recall Bruce Babbitt's call for voters to stand up for taxes and Pete duPont's challenge to Bob Dole to sign a no-tax pledge.

Over the past three decades, primary debates have become more numerous and more varied in format. Candidates, seeking to break out from the pack, look for gimmicks and clever lines, ranging from Mondale's "Where's the beef?" to Bush's calling Pete duPont "Pierre" in 1988. Because so few voters directly view these encounters, the effect of spin control and post-debate coverage is even more crucial than with general election debates. Even radio debates (such as the 1980 Nashua Reagan-Bush encounter) become television events as the sound bites are replayed on the evening news. Yet, the primary debates also offer a laboratory for experimentation with different formats, which may better adapt to television than the traditional moderator-panelist-candidates format so ingrained in general election debates.

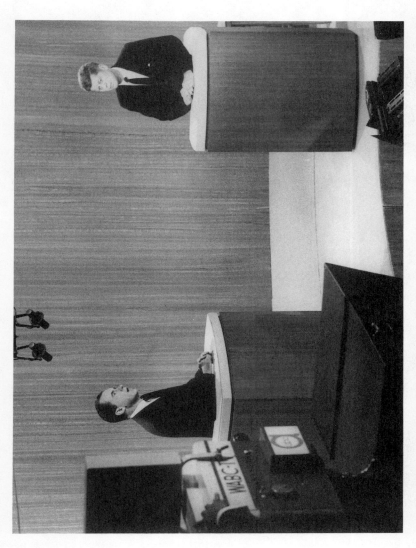

The four 1960 Kennedy-Nixon presidential debates, sponsored by the major commercial television networks, set the precedent for such encounters in future general election campaigns and played a significant role in John F. Kennedy's razor-thin victory over Richard Nixon. *(Photograph furnished courtesy of the Kennedy Library with permission of ABC)*

Sixteen years after the Kennedy-Nixon debates, Gerald Ford, an unelected incumbent trailing in the polls, and Jimmy Carter, a virtual unknown, were eager to debate one another. Their series of election debates represented the emergence of the League of Women Voters as a sponsor. *(Photograph provided courtesy of the League of Women Voters Education Fund)*

One week prior to the 1980 presidential election, Jimmy Carter finally engaged Ronald Reagan in a single debate in Cleveland, sponsored by the League of Women Voters. *(Photograph provided courtesy of the League of Women Voters Education Fund)*

League of Women Voters President Dot Ridings greets Walter Mondale and Ronald Reagan in one of two 1984 debates between the candidates. (*Photograph provided courtesy of the League of Women Voters Education Fund*)

George Bush and Michael Dukakis met at Wake Forest University for their first 1988 presidential debate, the first such event sponsored by the Commission on Presidential Debates. *(Susan Mullally Clark/Wake Forest University)*

Chapter Four

The Visual Dimension of Presidential Debates

The presidential debates are media events, solely TV events.
> —Professors Dan Nimmo and James E. Combs
> (1983, p. 67)

A medium is not simply an envelope that carries any letter; it is itself a major part of that message. . . . The important concept is that each medium, if its bias is properly exploited, reveals and communicates a unique aspect of reality, of truth.
> —Anthropologist Edmund Carpenter
> (1986, pp. 353, and 364)

In the age of television, the very nature of political persuasion had to change.
> —Political Scientist James David Barber
> (1980, p. 301)

Although presidential debates began as live confrontations before a specified audience in a designated place, contemporary debates are uniquely *major television events*. They are broadcast live to a mass audience, most of whom view them in the privacy of their own homes. Presidential debates have moved to what Susan Drucker terms *electronic public space*, and because the nature of debate changes with the context, this shift has produced "a new form of debate" (1989, pp. 7, 20).

The media, which has played a significant role in producing televised presidential debates, rationalizes its participation as public service based on its perceived mandate to provide coverage of live campaign events. Yet, as technical difficulties developed in the latter part of the first 1976

Ford and Carter debate, the candidates ignored the live audience, stopping the debate for twenty-eight minutes until audio was restored. "The lesson was clear: no media, no debate" (Nimmo & Combs, 1983, p. 67).

Clearly, to the extent that people experience presidential debates at all, they do so as televised events (Bulsys, 1989). "Nowadays, for all intents and purposes, political campaigns *happen* on television" (Armstrong, 1988, p. 29). As journalist Theodore White, in his capstone analysis of U.S. presidential campaigns from 1956 to 1980, observed, "American politics and television are now so completely locked together that it is impossible to tell the story of one without the other" (1982, p. 165). Yet, more than thirty years following the Kennedy and Nixon televised debates, scholars and media analysts continue to stress what is said in debates, the content, while virtually ignoring the unique features of the medium carrying that content to all receivers except for the handful able to attend debates in person.

This tendency to overemphasize content and underemphasize media is typical of most political communication scholarship. As communication scholar Kraus (1988, p. 15) chided, "Despite the growing influence of television . . . studies failed to seriously investigate the role of the media in electoral politics." Past research is grounded in the assumption that, to the extent that presidential debates influence receivers at all, they do so via their content.

If television manifests a unique symbol system, as James Chesebro (1984), Gavriel Salomon (1987), and other scholars suggest, it may fundamentally shape what is communicated to receivers, apart from the content. Such a prospect carries significant implications for any understanding of the nature and impact of presidential debates.

CONTEMPORARY TELEVISION IS A UNIQUE COMMUNICATION MEDIUM

Television has come a long way from its crude beginnings. Early television programming consisted of mostly live events, often shot with only two black and white cameras; news shows featured talking heads reading stories on camera. Contemporary television does a better job of exploiting the full potential of this medium, and as a result, has ushered in a "new language" in politics (Carpenter, 1986, p. 353). Contemporary television is a unique medium in part because it emphasizes visual content over verbal, and in part because it fosters viewer perceptions of an intimate connection between themselves and the people they come to know through television.

Television Stresses Visual Messages

Television communication consists of both verbal and visual components. "It encompasses what is said (the verbal message), what is shown (the visual message), and how it is presented (production techniques)" (Nesbit, 1988, p. 20). But, it is the visual component, a combination of what is shown and how it is presented, that renders television communication unique, even when compared to live presentations.

The visual component of television communication dwarfs the verbal dimension. Political consultant Ken Swope noted, "In order of importance on television come pictures, music, then words" (Kern, 1989, p. 35). Kraus observed, "With the adoption of the visual dimension, this new medium was believed to be more powerful than other communication media" (1988, p. 13). Other research refers to "the primacy of the visual over the audio channel" (Burgoon, 1980; Graber, 1987; Paletz & Guthrie, 1987, p. 20). Political scientist Michael Robinson noted, "Television has an audio-visual quality the other media lack. Most of the research in the field indicates that this obvious and unique quality makes the content of television more memorable and evocative" (1978, p. 19).

As a result of its visual component, television communicates a unique type of message. Media scholar Joshua Meyrowitz characterized television communication as (1) more expressive, featuring the use of kinesic and vocalic nonverbal elements in communication—receivers use expressive messages to form impressions about communicators; (2) more presentational, bearing a physical resemblance to the object being characterized—receivers employ presentational messages to form mental images of things; and (3) more analogic, involving continuous messages—receivers use analogic messages to determine how the communicator feels about them and/or their relationship (1985, pp. 93–97). He adds that such messages "have different possibilities and limitations" (1985, p. 97).

One such difference involves relative receiver involvement in message processing. Because television communication relies more heavily on a "pictorial symbol system" (Salomon, 1981, p. 205) it requires less active involvement by receivers in message processing (Chesebro, 1984; Graber, 1987; Krugman, 1971; Salomon, 1979, 1981; Wright, 1974). Reduced receiver involvement does not undermine comprehension and retention of visual images. As Jamieson concluded, "Visual images are more quickly comprehended and more readily retained than verbal ones" (1988, p. 114).

Television, however, may not be the appropriate medium to communicate specific information. On the one hand, less active involvement is not well suited to the cognitive processing of verbal messages. For example, researchers in social psychology report that especially print messages, but also audio messages, require more active receiver involvement in message processing than video messages, thus increasing the role and importance of content in the process of influence (Chaiken & Eagly, 1976, 1983; Keating & Latane, 1976). Television, which features both video and audio, involves less active message processing because of the presence of the visual dimension. In addition, research suggests that visual messages distract receivers, interfering with verbal processing, thus inhibiting the learning of nonvisual content (Gunter, 1980; Paletz & Guthrie, 1987; Warshaw, 1978).

Over time television has shifted to an increasing reliance on visual messages, in large part to fully capitalize on the medium's unique communication potential. One manifestation of this development involves television advertising, where Charles Larson (1982), Jamieson (1988), and others point to a rather pronounced movement away from message content and toward message technique. Journalist Eric Clark further documented this trend:

The move away from product-oriented, "reason why" ads was encouraged by the growth of television as a major advertising medium. By its nature, television is better able to convey images than facts. . . . By the mid-1970s less than half of American television commercials could be regarded as informative even using the very generous definition that they contained just one of fourteen different information criteria. (1988, p. 69)

Television's proclivity toward visual messages has exerted a profound impact on American politics. During the past thirty years, as television displaced alternative communication modalities in political communication, the visual message overtook the verbal message in political discourse. As Jamieson puts it, "Increasingly political eloquence is visual, not verbal" (1988, p. 44). Neil Postman continues:

In the age of TV . . . the visual image . . . has now emerged as our basic unit of political conversation. Politics today is not *The Federalist* or *The Federalist Papers*. It is not the Lincoln-Douglas debates. It is not even Roosevelt's fireside chats. In all of these, language was the central ingredient. In the age of TV, the ideas of political leaders are not susceptible either to refutation or logical analysis, any more than are McDonald's commercials. (1988, p. 13)

The dominance of visual over verbal messages in television communication makes sense out of the results of Thomas Patterson and Robert McClure's seminal study of television news coverage during the 1972 presidential campaign. They found that because television news communicates visually and political campaign issues are not easily depicted pictorially, television news provides very limited issue information; as a result, television news viewers are less informed (1976, pp. 54–55).

Television Fosters a Perception of Intimacy

Television's emphasis on visual communication is the basis for a another unique feature of this medium. Namely, television fosters a perception of intimacy with a source unattainable via any other communication modality except for interpersonal.

Receivers respond more intimately to television for two reasons. First, television's reliance on visual messages, coupled with its capacity to project close-ups, affords close, personal access to a communicator's facial cues (Brummett, 1988; Gold, 1988; Keating & Latane, 1976). However, it is not the close-up alone, but the close-up in tandem with the relatively small viewing screen, that affords the illusion of intimate contact with a source. As Meyrowitz explained, it is "the relative size of the figure within the frame" that causes a heightened perception of facial cues (1986, p. 257). Or, as Brummett observed, "Its small screen allows television to focus on the interpersonal: close-up shots are more successful on the television screen than they would be on the cinema screen" (1988, pp. 210–11).

The illusion of intimate contact is magnified by the fact that the television viewer can stare at the communicator's face at length, something that would be considered rude in a dyadic context, hence discouraged. As David Altheide and Robert Snow observed, "With television, the viewer is allowed the anonymity to read faces intensely" (1979, p. 39). Thus, in commenting about the impact of television on American politics, Kraus maintained that, the prolonged close-up "supplied vivid, intimate sketches of candidates as they campaigned" (1988, p. 115).

Because it affords access to the human face, television, like interpersonal communication, places greater emphasis on expression in communication (Kern, 1989; Meyrowitz, 1985, 1986; Newcomb, 1982; Perse & Rubin, 1989; Robinson, 1978). As Meyrowitz stated, "On television, expressions usually dominate words" (1985, p. 103).

A second reason why receivers respond more intimately to television concerns the viewing context. Most people view television in the private confines of their homes, literally inviting communicators into their living or family rooms. Television's use in the home accents its more intimate nature (Brummett, 1988). Political advertising guru Tony Schwartz labeled television as "a private, 'undress' medium" (Kaid & Davidson, 1986, p. 185). Further, Richard Armstrong commented, "Politics is something you do in the privacy of your own house, with your T-shirt on, with a beer in your hands, with your shoes off. It's like belching. That's where television has left us" (1988, p. 32).

Television gives the impression of being socially present, which also contributes to a perception of intimacy (Beniger, 1987; Keating & Latane, 1976). Such an *appearance* of a one-on-one relationship involving a source and a receiver resembles the interpersonal context (Levy, 1979; Rubin & McHugh, 1987). As a result, Donald Horton and Richard Wohl initially posited that television is responsible for the development of "parasocial relationships" between television personalities and viewers that generate the "illusion of a traditional face-to-face relationship" (1956, p. 215). Elizabeth Perse and Rebecca Rubin add that "like social relationships, parasocial relationships develop over a period of time and are enhanced when media presentations resemble interpersonal interaction" (1989, p. 60). James Beniger (1987) depicted this as "pseudo-communal communications." Perse and Rubin maintained, "Parasocial interaction is a normal consequence of television viewing."

Television is perceived as a more intimate medium. Thus, it rewards a very different pattern of communication techniques than alternative modalities. Indeed, television's intimacy, more than any other single factor, has produced the changes in political discourse that Jamieson (1988) laments. Television penalizes those techniques traditionally prized in public speaking (e.g., carefully chosen prose, well-reasoned and supported arguments, the ability to rouse large audiences, etc.) and rewards those techniques most prized in interpersonal communication (e.g., nonverbal techniques like facial cues that communicate warmth, body position that suggests immediacy, or vocal cues that indicate trustworthiness) (Atkinson, 1984; Pfau, 1990).

The remainder of this chapter examines the impact of the television medium on the nature of presidential debates. Because of the uniqueness of television, we discover that the medium has altered the manner in which politicians must communicate in debates. As James Barber concludes, "In the age of television, the very nature of political persuasion had to change" (1980, p. 301). It did, and the remainder of this chapter examines the precise nature of these changes.

IMPACT OF THE VISUAL DIMENSION: A MACRO VIEW

Television alters the manner that influence is exercised, requiring candidates to adjust to the idiosyncrasies of adapting their communication techniques to the biases of television. In one experimental study, Akiba Cohen (1976) found that some candidates used television more effectively than others. In a retrospective assessment of candidate influence and television in presidential campaigns from 1960 to 1976, William Adams (1983) reported that reliance on television was beneficial to Kennedy in 1960, Goldwater in 1964, Nixon and Wallace in 1968, and Carter in 1976, with the advantage most pronounced among more educated and more independent voters.

What is it about the communication of candidates that can enhance or retard their effectiveness with television, especially in televised presidential debates? This section takes a macro view of the impact of the visual dimension of television on presidential debates.

Undermines the Verbal Component of Debates

Television's emphasis on visual messages and its intimate communication have combined to undermine the verbal component of political communication, including presidential debates. Is the verbal component important? Yes—verbal messages, rather than visual messages, are required to communicate effectively about issue content. Issue content requires communication about both problems as well as solutions. Although problems can be depicted visually, typically solutions cannot. Take, for example, the 1988 television messages in support of George Bush. One depicted a revolving prison door; another, featuring the infamous Willie Horton, graphically portrayed problems related to crime and punishment. Similarly, most past presidential campaigns have employed powerful visual messages to direct the public's attention to problems, such as inflation, unemployment, the environment, corruption in government, and threats to national security. Television excels in this area because problems manifest symptoms that can be concretely depicted using visual images.

Communication about solutions to problems requires words and reasoned arguments; television is not well suited to either. Political scholar Austin Ranney (1983, p. 182) explains that television carries the potential to lull receivers to sleep because it substitutes direct experiences for thinking and for words. Or, as David Webster, U.S. Director of the

British Broadcasting Corporation, put it, "Television . . . happens to be better as a medium of experience, than as a medium of exposition. It is not actually very good at explaining things" (Linsky, 1983, p. 18).

The important issue content of political discourse concerns what candidates recommend as solutions to the important problems facing the nation. Such content is intrinsically abstract and intricate, and as a result, is communicated more effectively via words than pictures (Patterson, 1980). Past president of the American Council of Learned Societies, John William Ward, has astutely observed television's bias toward simplification, a characteristic which "makes it a difficult medium for conveying complexity and ambiguity" (Linsky, 1983, p. 12).

The verbal content that television does provide consists of short, condensed speech, resembling sloganeering more than rational discourse. Jamieson (1988) and Jamieson and Birdsell (1988) have documented this trend historically. Jamieson and Birdsell maintain, "Since the advent of the broadcast media, the length of political messages has decreased steadily" (1988, p. 96). The authors referred to contemporary televised debates, in particular, as "a gladiatorial contest in miniature" (1988, p. 118). They commented:

> Rather than eliciting depth, the format [of televised debates] invites sloganeering. Brief answers on a shower of topics creates an informational blur. The press panel asks questions designed to elicit news headlines, not information of use to voters. The superficial is rewarded; the substantive, spurned. (1988, p. 119)

Jamieson (1988, pp. 10–11) notes that the format employed in the 1984 Reagan and Mondale debates resulted in candidate responses on any one topic that ranged from one to two-and-one-half minutes in length. (By contrast, Lincoln and Douglas spoke for ninety minutes on each topic in their 1858 debates.)

The tendency toward condensed, superficial verbal discourse has been compounded by a trend toward anecdotes as the supporting data of choice in contemporary debates. Because debates are televised events, effective stories carry more probative force for viewers than hard evidence. The use of anecdotal support is best illustrated in Ronald Reagan's debating style. Jamieson maintained that Reagan often employed anecdotes as the basis for his argumentative claims, and that while anecdotes fail to meet traditional standards of probity, Reagan's credibility caused receivers to "suspend disbelief" and accept his assertions "without rigorous testing" (1988, pp. 151–52). Communication scholar Ellen Reid Gold further observed that Reagan's "logic is . . . that of oral cultures, for a single anecdote serves as adequate evidence for a conclusion" (1988, p. 170).

The increasing use of anecdotal support undermines political argument. Two Canadian scholars (Kymlicka & Matthews) granted the effectiveness of stories in political discourse, but warned that "if the thinker *thinks* in anecdotes, this may lead to a dangerous oversimplification of what are, in reality, very complex matters" (1988, p. 23). Television, because it communicates through narrative and drama, encourages political communicators to conceptualize public policy through its visual logic, rather than though abstract symbols.

Presidential debate rhetoric in the era of television is "short and quotable—catchy if you will" (Reinsch, 1988, p. 300). It consists of assertions, brief claims which, when supported at all, are backed with colorful anecdotes. The verbal discourse that television features is virtually devoid of substance in a traditional sense. As Jamieson concluded, "Labels are no longer a tendency in politics. In this electronic age, they are our politics" (1988, p. 248).

Television devalues content in campaign discourse, instead stressing candidate image, a by-product of the importance of the visual emphasis in television communication. Postman argues that "television . . . does not direct attention to ideas, which are abstract, sequential, slowmoving, and complex. It directs us to respond to images, which are holistic, concrete, and simplistic. That is why it rarely matters what anyone says on television" (1988, p. 18). Scott Keeter concurs:

The importance of candidate images—relative to other information—may be greater for voters who depend on television. . . . Television by its nature provides a qualitatively different product. It provides the candidate as a person. This is a function of the visual and *actual* nature of television's content, and is reinforced by the practices of news organizations and personnel that serve to downplay cognitive content. (1987, p. 345)

This is consistent with Marshall McLuhan's (1964) characterization of television as a cool, low-intensity medium. Images are less involving, less intense. Herbert Asher noted, "The emphasis on 'cool' images may result in appeals to the electorate that are based less on issue considerations and more on style" (1980, p. 240). Or, as Richard Nixon reflected, "In the television age a candidate's appearance and style count for more than his ideas and record" (Berry, 1987, p. 37).

Keeter (1987) referred specifically to the imagery of the 1960 Kennedy and Nixon debates. Other analysts agree. Joseph Berry refers to the 1960 debates as having "crystallized to a battle of appearances and images" (1987, p. 35). Or, as J. Leonard Reinsch explained: "The next day, few could recite exactly what was said during the debate. But Kennedy projected the 'feel' of a winner. He had enhanced his image—and image won out over content" (1988, p. 143). In reflecting on how viewers use political debates, Meyrowitz observed, "When most people think back on such televised debates they tend to remember the general style and emotional state of the participants rather than their specific verbal arguments" (1985, p. 100).

Promotes a New Style of Political Discourse

For better or worse, television has changed the nature of political discourse. The unique biases of the medium promote a new style of political communication that enhances the impact of source factors; requires a more personal, casual style on the part of speakers; elevates the role and impact of the nonverbal stream; and demands the use of positive relational messages. This section explores each of these elements.

Enhances the Impact of Source Factors. Television, because it places a higher premium on presentational factors in political communication, is responsible for the ascendancy of character as the dominant criterion for assessing communicators (Rudd, 1986). In a recent study that compared television with other media and communication modalities, Pfau (1990) reported that source factors were responsible for more influence on receivers than content in television and interpersonal communication, whereas content was more impactful in radio, print, and public address communication. These findings held for commercial, political, and social action message categories.

Meyrowitz attributed the primacy of source factors in television communication to the electronic media's ability to " 'capture' personal attributes" (1985, p. 102). As Keeter noted, "Candidate personal qualities became more important for television dependent voters during the 1960s" (1987, p. 344). A wealth of data over the past two decades concerning voter decision criteria points increasingly to the primacy of character over issue content (Asher, 1980; Campbell, 1983; DeVries & Tarrance, 1972; Graber, 1980a; Hahn & Goncher, 1972; Kirkpatrick, Lyons & Fitzgerald, 1975; O'Keefe, 1975; Pomper, 1975; Shapiro, 1969).

Television's visual capacity has served as the catalyst for the growing influence of candidate source factors in political communication. Television enhances source factors by generating viewer perceptions of close, intimate contact with candidates. Gladys Lang and Kurt Lang (1968) maintain that this medium's visual dimension promotes a sense of intimacy between candidate and viewer naturally lending itself to emphasis on personal qualities. Keating and Latane noted that television can produce "greater liking" because it conveys the character and style of a communicator (1976, p. 126). Schram argued that "the camera provides the crucial, close, personal insights into the candidates" (1987, p. 308). Adams explained, "Candidate persona in the fullest, richest, and most vivid sense can be conveyed only through television" (1983, p. 168). Gold posits that the elements of the speaker-audience relationship resemble the interpersonal context, and "operate more forcefully in public rhetoric than we had realized" (1988, p. 172).

Television also enhances source factors by undermining the role of content in political communication. Political scientist Doris Graber argued that television's absence of content "left the television viewer with information weighted heavily in favor of using characteristics of the man, rather than issue positions, as voting criteria" (1976, pp. 300–301). Similarly, Joseph Wagner (1983) posited that television suppresses the viewer's ability or inclination to make substantive distinctions between candidates. In commenting on presidential debates specifically, Edwin Diamond and Kathleen Friery observed:

> Television is an information-poor medium: facts, statistics, charges, and counter-charges fly past the viewer, often too rapidly to be digested. But because television is at the same time an emotion-rich medium, qualities of appearance such as "competence" and "trustworthiness" are easier to pick out. The media, by steering away from the facts, reinforce this process. (1987, p. 49)

Research on information processing provides theoretical support for the proposition that television elevates person variables in persuasive communication. The heuristic model indicates that, under certain circumstances, "people exert little cognitive effort in judging the validity of a persuasive message and, instead, may base their agreement with a message on a rather superficial assessment of a variety of extrinsic persuasion cues," such as communicator characteristics (Chaiken, 1987, p. 3). Media is one such circumstance (Petty, Cacioppo & Kasmer, 1988), particularly when the personal salience of a message is low. Television requires limited receiver involvement in message processing (Krugman, 1965; Wright, 1974), which has the effect of increasing the impact of source factors in persuasion (Burnkrant & Sawyer, 1983; Chaiken, 1980; Graber, 1987; Haynes, 1988; Petty & Cacioppo, 1984; Petty, Cacioppo & Goldman, 1981; Petty, Cacioppo & Schumann, 1983; Rhine & Severance, 1970).

The implication for presidential debates is that television viewers are inclined to use them to make judgments of candidate character and not to increase their store of information about candidate positions on issues. Television is a visual medium, and as a result, television's rhetoric is source oriented. As Graber observed, "When candidates for political office are shown on the television screen, audiences tend to use the pictures to judge the candidates' personality traits such as competence, integrity, leadership, and empathy" (1987, p. 77).

Most people who view televised presidential debates render holistic judgments of candidate performance, and what they see more than the content that they hear plays the most decisive role. This claim draws support from a large number of studies indicating that viewing presidential debates primarily affected perceptions of candidate image or personality: in 1960 (Katz & Feldman, 1977; Lang & Lang, 1977; Lubell, 1977; Rosenthal, 1963); in 1976 (Becker, Pepper, Wenner & Kim, 1979; Bowes & Strentz, 1979; Casey & Fitzgerald, 1977; Davis, 1979; Morrow, 1977; Smith, 1977; Walker & Petersen, 1981); in 1980 (Berquist & Golden, 1981; Brydon, 1985b; Davis, 1982; Vancil & Pendell, 1984); and in 1984 (Pfau, 1987; Reinsch, 1988). The question of debate effects is examined in much more detail in Chapter 5.

Rewards a More Personal, Casual Communication. As we noted previously, television is an intimate medium. It electronically transports communicators into the private confines of viewers' homes; because it affords immediate access to facial cues, television generates the illusion of interpersonal contact with communicators. In turn, television's intimacy rewards a more personal, casual communication.

Television has changed the way candidates are expected to communicate. The medium ushered in "a new eloquence," featuring a softer, warmer, communication, more similar to the interpersonal context (Atkinson, 1984; Jamieson, 1988, p. 56; Levy, 1979). As Joe McGinniss observed two decades ago, "The success of any TV performer depends on his achieving a low-pressure style of presentation. . . . The TV politician cannot make a speech; he must engage in intimate conversation. He must never press. He should suggest, not state; request, not demand" (1969, pp. 29–30).

The days of old-fashioned political oratory, replete with lengthy, well-reasoned, impassioned appeals, are gone. Such techniques do not work on television. Max Atkinson argues that traditional oratory is designed for a specific communication context, not for television. It features performance, which when employed on television, comes across as "overdone, overacted, over-prepared, over-rehearsed, and generally lacking in spontaneity—qualities that have not been particularly effective in coming to terms with the viewing and listening requirements of living-room audiences" (1986, p. 41). Ranney further explains:

Most observers agree that the kind of personality, appearance, and speaking style that inspires standing ovations from crowds of thousands in auditoriums is quite different from the kind that inspires liking and confidence from a few people sitting in front of a television set in their own homes. The auditorium situation calls for a commanding presence, a strong voice projected at a high volume, large gestures, and dramatic punch lines with plenty of pauses for cheers. The TV-room situation calls for a pleasant and friendly presence, a moderate tone of voice, small and natural gestures, and a general conversational manner. (1983, p. 103)

The old oratory is too hot for television communication. "The old eloquence, which spoke in metaphors of battle and fire, was contentious, passionate, and intense" (Jamieson, 1988, p. 45). Political consultant Joseph Napolitan adds that "television works best if it is low-key, soft-sell" (1972, p. 85). The new discourse seeks to establish a relationship with viewers, and this demands an informal communication style (Perse & Rubin, 1989).

McGinniss identified Hubert Humphrey as the epitome of the old eloquence, noting that "he became lethal in a television studio" (1969, p. 30). Even though John Kennedy was the first presidential candidate with a communication style that adapted well to the television era, "perceived as a cool candidate on a cool medium: television" (Berry, 1987, p. 36), Ronald Reagan is the epitome of the new discourse.

Reagan has been characterized as the great communicator, due to his ability to adapt his communication style to the specific demands of each communication modality. Lou Cannon comments, "He knew how to make a speech and how to deliver a punch line. He knew that it was necessary to look directly into the television camera without bobbing his head, and he knew how to give a concise answer that compressed easily into a fifteen-second sound bite" (1991, p. 40). Reagan's television style was more conversational in nature, thus ideally suited for this communication medium. Journalists Peter Goldman and Tony Fuller, who covered the 1984 presidential campaign for *Newsweek*, observed that Reagan "did not have the elegance of a Winston Churchill or an Adlai Stevenson. . . . He had instead a gift of intimacy, of plain speech, simple vision, and open feelings. . . . His command of the medium was instinctive and sure" (1985, p. 29).

Jamieson argues that Reagan is a consummate conversationalist, also employing "an unprecedented level of self-disclosure," thus engendering affection from other people (1988, p. 165). This is precisely the communication style that television both demands and rewards. Schram characterizes Reagan's success with television, noting, "He skillfully mastered the ability to step through the television tubes and join Americans in their living rooms" (1987, p. 26).

Reagan's personal and casual style served him well in four general election debates, two in 1980 (one with John Anderson and one with Jimmy Carter) and two in 1984. His colloquial, low-key performance in 1980 undermined Jimmy Carter's attempt to characterize him as an extremist and as a warmonger (Smith, 1980). In response to repeated attacks by Carter about his positions, Reagan smiled, tossed his head, and responded, "There you go again" (Smith, 1980).

The same style helped him overcome doubts about whether he was too old to serve another term; these first surfaced following Reagan's mediocre performance against Walter Mondale in the first 1984 debate. In the second debate, Reagan succeeded in brushing aside doubts about his age with the simple quip, "I am not going to exploit, for political purposes, my opponent's youth and inexperience" (Magnuson & Church, 1984, p. 22). Reinsch noted that "with one joke, Reagan demolished the age issue" (1988, p. 289). Reporter John Dillin, commenting on Reagan's appeal to the television audience in the second debate, observed:

The most revealing difference of all [between Reagan's live and televised image] was the faces of the two men. Reagan's face, as seen on TV, is expressive. The President doesn't just speak with words. He speaks with a frown, a smile, or an expression of "aw shucks." In the press balcony, what seemed like a pause was actually a moment in which Reagan was saying, with a facial expression or a head movement, "Why me?" or "How could you say that?" His eyes are lively, his cheeks are pink, and all this comes through in living color on television. Mondale's face, as seen on TV, is unexpressive. (1984, p. 3)

Elevates the Role and Impact of the Nonverbal Stream. The more personal, casual communication that contemporary television demands elevates the nonverbal stream in political discourse. As indicated previously, television affords the viewer prolonged access to the human face, thus emphasizing expressiveness in human communication (Kern, 1989; Meyrowitz, 1985, 1986; Newcomb, 1982; Perse & Rubin, 1989; Robinson, 1978).

The nonverbal stream, which exerts more impact than verbal content in interpersonal communication (Argyle, Alkema & Gilmour, 1971; McMahan, 1976; Mehrabian, 1971), should exert more impact in television influence as well. The reason is the same in both instances: the unique capacity of the interpersonal channel to promote intimacy, and of television to foster the perception of intimacy, between communicators and receivers (Beniger, 1987; Horton & Wohl, 1956; Keating & Latane, 1976). Altheide and Snow argued that "given the close-up potential of the television camera, the audience comes to rely on facial gestures as the determining factor in identifying the intentions and motives of the characters" (1979, p. 38).

The role of the nonverbal stream in television communication may explain the failure of political communication scholars to detect large debate effects (see Chapter 5). Most such studies are geared more to the verbal stream, attempting to assess the impact of what candidates say. If, by contrast, most of the meaning of a communication event is carried via the nonverbal stream, as some communication scholars have advocated (Argyle, Alkema & Gilmour, 1971; Argyle, Salter, Nicholson, Williams & Burgess, 1970; Birdwhistell, 1955; Burgoon, Buller & Woodall, 1989; Gitter, Black & Fishman, 1975; Philpott, 1983), then investigators may be looking in the wrong place and/or employing the wrong tools in their search for political debate effects (Kaid & Davidson, 1986; Kelley & Mirer, 1974).

Communication scholars have just begun to explore the full impact of nonverbal cues in political influence. Keating and Latane (1976), Graber (1987), and Meyrowitz (1985) maintain that the nonverbal stream carries considerable impact in political influence. Graber (1987) claims that viewers rely on pictorial images of candidates to frame judgments about their personalities. In two studies using university students as voters and one using "average adults," Rosenberg, Bohan, McCafferty, and Harris found that photographic depictions of hypothetical candidates influence receiver images of candidates and receiver voting disposition. The researchers conclude: "The results indicate a strong and consistent effect of appearance" (1986, p. 117).

The impact of the nonverbal stream in presidential debate influence has received scant attention to date. Jamieson (1988) and Jamieson and Birdsell (1988) maintained that debates provide information to viewers about the nature of candidates, and that much of this information is carried via the nonverbal stream. Carlin (1989) claimed that a candidate's nonverbal skills play an important role in communicating leadership, while Hinck (1988) argued that the primary function of presidential debates is to facilitate viewer judgments about leadership potential. Jamieson and Birdsell concluded that "some of the evidence we gain [about candidates' personalities] is nonverbal," including our judgments about crucial credibility traits "such as competence, integrity, leadership, and empathy" (1988, p. 144). Lois Wingerson (1982) maintained that although polling data does not reflect it, nonverbal cues exert a significant influence on our judgments about candidates and their performances in debates.

Actual data on the relative impact of the nonverbal stream in presidential debates is limited, somewhat contradictory, and heavily anecdotal. Katz and Feldman (1977) suggested that candidate style, which is a function of how they appeared on television, worked to the benefit of John Kennedy in the 1960 debates. Berry (1987) maintained that Kennedy projected a more attractive image in the first 1960 debate, while former CBS News executive Sig Mickelson concluded that in the first 1960 debate Richard Nixon came across to television viewers as "pale and uncomfortable," Kennedy as "robust and healthy" (1989, p. 122).

The claim that Kennedy's appearance was responsible for his superior performance in the first 1960 debate is often documented with reference to data which indicates that most people who heard the debate on radio thought Nixon had won, whereas most who saw it on television thought Kennedy had won (Lang & Lang, 1984, p. 205; Mickelson, 1989, p. 121; Ranney, 1983, p. 15; Twentieth Century Fund Task Force on Televised Presidential Debates, 1979, p. 44). However, Vancil and Pendell (1987) carefully examined the original data, finding it wanting. They concluded that claims of a Nixon radio victory should be rejected because "none of the evidence in support of it withstands close scrutiny" (1987, p. 24). Vancil and Pendell do not attempt to argue that candidate appearance is unimportant as an influence on voter perceptions. They simply posit that the 1960 data used to document the claim that Kennedy's appearance tipped the balance in the first debate is suspect (1987, p. 25).

One investigation does suggest that nonverbal cues may be overrated in debate influence. An experimental study by Krauss, Apple, Morency, Wenzel, and Winton (1981) reported that when people were asked to render a judgment about candidates based on excerpts from the 1976 Mondale and Dole vice-presidential debate, they relied more heavily on the verbal stream.

Nonetheless, the early research points to an important role for candidate nonverbal cues in presidential debate influence. Contradicting the Krauss et al. study, Sauter (1990) argued that Dole's nonverbals in his debate were largely responsible for his ineffectiveness. In analyzing Dole's "acerbic comments," Sauter posited that Dole's humor, which was usually effective in live appearances, failed him in the television debate because he delivered his remarks without a smile and because reaction shots of the audience were not shown on television (1990, pp. 59–60).

Wingerson (1982) found that the visual depiction of Carter's tension was a major reason for his perceived loss to Reagan in the 1980 presidential debate. Turning the coin, Blankenship, Marlene Fine, and Leslie Davis (1983) and Jamieson and Birdsell (1988, p. 146) attributed Reagan's victory in the 1980 debate to his "self-effacing humor, his genial ability to disarm, and his capacity to reassure." Similarly, a Dartmouth group studying the 1980 Reagan and Carter debate reported that facial displays exerted a significant impact on viewers' attitudes and perceptions about Carter's performance (reported in Wingerson, 1982). Ritter and Henry argued that Carter's attacks in the 1980 debate were ineffective in part because he "failed to coordinate his nonverbal behavior with his verbal messages" (1990, p. 83).

Journalist William Henry argued that Walter Mondale's strong showing in his first 1984 debate with Ronald Reagan was due to the fact that he was able to project a warm persona, while Geraldine Ferraro lost the 1984 vice-presidential debate because of her "chilly demeanor." Henry wrote, "Her ready smile and quick humor had been replaced by a stern, slightly abrasive, lawyerly manner and a thin-lipped, almost petulant grimace" (1985, p. 253). Finally, Decker's analysis of the 1988 Quayle and Bentsen vice-presidential debate suggested that the candidates' nonverbals helped determine viewer impressions of both men (1990, p. 179).

Requires Positive Relational Messages. Just as television elevates the role of the nonverbal stream in communication, it also places a premium on positive relational messages (Chesebro, 1984). What are relational messages? What role do relational messages play in presidential debates? This section attempts to answer both questions.

Jurgen Ruesch and Gregory Bateson (1951) and subsequently Paul Watzlawick, Janet Beavin, and Don Jackson (1967) initially posited that all communication contains both report and command dimensions. Whereas the report dimension contains the specific content communicated, the command or relational dimension "indicate[s] how two or more people regard each other, regard their relationship, or regard themselves within the context of the relationship" (Burgoon & Hale, 1984, p. 193).

Relational messages are an intrinsic feature of all human communication. When Watzlawick, Beavin, and Jackson claimed that "one cannot *not* communicate," they meant that when we communicate, we are always sending relational messages, no matter what might be happening with respect to content (1967, p. 49). The relational message dimension is inherent in all cases where communication modality makes possible either real contact, as in interpersonal communication, or perceived contact, as in television, between a source and receiver (Burgoon, 1980; Burgoon & Hale, 1987). The reason is that both interpersonal and television communication stress the visual channel, coupled with close, personal access to a source's facial cues, which accent the nonverbal stream.

Relational messages can be communicated verbally, as when one says to another, "I like you." More often, however, they are communicated nonverbally, often accompanying some verbal message (Burgoon, Buller, Hale & deTurck, 1984; Newton, Burgoon & Traynowicz, 1989; Sillars, Pike, Jones & Murphy, 1984). And, since communication modalities vary in their capacity to carry nonverbal messages (Burns & Beier, 1973; Keating & Latane, 1976; Meyrowitz, 1985), the relative impact of relational, as opposed to content, messages is more pronounced in interpersonal and television communication (Pfau, 1990).

The limited research concerning the impact of relational messages in persuasion suggests that messages communicating more positive relational ratings—more similarity/depth, equality, immediacy/affection, composure, receptivity/trust, and less dominance and formality—facilitate influence, with the receptivity/trust dimension exerting the most impact (Burgoon, Pfau, Parrott, Birk, Coker & Burgoon, 1987).

The emphasis on positive relational messages is consistent with what is known about political influence, especially in a televised debate setting. We have previously documented the emphasis on intimacy and expressiveness in televised political communication (Graber, 1981, 1987; Jamieson, 1988; Jamieson & Birdsell, 1988; Keating & Latane, 1976; Kern, 1989; Kingdon, 1966; Lang & Lang, 1968; McGinniss, 1969; Meyrowitz, 1985; Nesbit, 1988; Schram, 1987; Wagner, 1983). Robert Abelson (cited in Leo, 1984) indicates that the communication of warm feelings is three to four times more powerful than traditional candidate preference criteria such as party identification or issues.

Martel (1983, p. 83) maintains that a candidate's smile is important in communicating confidence, control, and friendliness, and that smiles have played a role in past presidential debates, contributing to Kennedy's success against Nixon in 1960 and to Reagan's performances against both Anderson and Carter in 1980. Jamieson (1988) claims that Reagan's speaking style communicates trust, affection, and similarity, important relational messages. Oft-Rose (1989) stresses the importance of relational messages in presidential debates, noting that many viewers of the first Bush and Dukakis debate who thought Michael Dukakis got the better of George Bush on the arguments nonetheless rated Bush as the more likable communicator, thus militating against any Dukakis advantage in the debate.

In the only experimental study of relational messages in televised presidential debates, Pfau and Kang concluded of the first 1988 debate, "For both candidates, and across all attitude measures, more positive relational ratings enhanced influence" (1989, pp. 27–28). Communication of greater immediacy/affection (consisting of warmth, involvement, enthusiasm, and a sense of personal interest in the receiver), equality (comprising a cooperative attitude, a sense of similarity, and the absence of a superior attitude), similarity/depth (including caring and friendliness), receptivity/trust (consisting of sincerity, honesty, interest in communicating, and willingness to listen), and composure (comprising comfort, poise, relaxation, and lack of tension) positively rated to candidate influence, accounting for substantial variance in most dependent measures (Pfau & Kang, 1989).

IMPACT OF THE VISUAL DIMENSION: A MICRO VIEW

Contemporary presidential debates are uniquely television events (Bulsys, 1989; Nimmo & Combs, 1983), and television has made a lasting imprint on the nature and impact of presidential debates (Drucker, 1989).

This chapter suggests that television is a unique medium, and, as Carpenter (1986), Salomon (1987), Jamieson (1984, 1988), and others argue, is itself a major part of what is communicated. Television communication promotes visual messages over verbal ones, and visual messages are a combination of what is shown in conjunction with how it is presented (Jamieson, 1988; Kern, 1989; Nesbit, 1988). Nimmo (1970) viewed televised presidential debates as a confrontation of visual images.

This section focuses on issues relating to the staging and production of televised presidential debates, examining the nature and impact of camera treatment and candidate strategies as they pertain to visual image. Visual image bears the unique stamp of television, and it is an important matter, for as research by Shawn Rosenberg and Patrick McCafferty has demonstrated, different pictures of the same person produce quite different images.

Relatively minor changes in photographic presentation can produce significant differences in how a person is perceived. "Such changes . . . affect both the degree to which an individual is perceived to be fit for public office and the degree to which he is perceived to possess those qualities (competence, integrity, and likableness) that other research has shown to be relevant to voters' evaluations of political candidates" (1987, p. 37).

Camera Treatment and Visual Image

Cameras are the eyes of television. The camera techniques employed in producing a debate ultimately determine what the people sitting in their family or living rooms actually see when viewing a televised debate. A number of issues concerning camera techniques have been examined in past research.

One issue concerns camera angle and placement. Tiemens examined a variety of camera treatment factors, such as camera angle, camera framing, compositional balance, camera placement, image size, and asymmetry, in the 1976 Carter-Ford presidential debates. Tiemens reported that the differences in pictorial treatment of the candidates generally favored Carter, but that "these differences were subtle . . . and to most observers may have been imperceptible" (1978, p. 370). In the only visual analysis of a primary debate, Hellweg and Phillips (1981b) used Tiemens' methodology in examining the 1980 debate between Reagan and Bush in Houston. Their results showed that camera treatment was relatively even for the two contenders.

A study by Kepplinger and Donsbach filmed a West German politician at various angles in an attempt to determine whether it made any difference in viewer attitudes. The results indicated that the most favorable impressions were generated at eye level, generating such positive impressions as "natural," "likable," and "intelligent" (1987, p. 67).

Another issue involves camera treatment in conjunction with candidate behaviors to the camera. Four studies (Davis, 1978; Frye & Bryski, 1978; Frye, Goldhaber & Bryski, 1981; Tiemens, 1978) examined camera angle and eye gaze during the 1976 Ford-Carter and 1980 Carter-Reagan debates. Davis (1978) found that Carter appealed more directly to the public through the camera during his speaking time, whereas Ford focused more on the panelists, although this varied somewhat across the debates, whereas Frye and Bryski reported that Ford spoke to the camera more than his opponent, but that the difference was largely a function of his slower speaking rate. They also indicated that there was very little difference in the camera shots of the two candidates as they were speaking. One reason for Tiemens' (1978) conclusion that the 1976 debates favored Carter was that Carter achieved more eye contact with the camera than Ford.

Frye, Goldhaber, and Bryski (1981) reported that during the 1980 debate, both Carter and Reagan tended to look more at the panelists except for their closing statements where Carter gazed at the panelists and Reagan focused on the camera. In addition, they found that Carter was given more close-up camera treatment than Reagan during his summation, but that on balance the camera treatment benefited neither of the candidates.

One of the hottest issues involving camera techniques, and a persistent subject for negotiation prior to debates and complaints following debates, involves the use of reaction shots, depiction of one candidate while the other candidate is speaking. Herbert Seltz and Richard Yoakam (1977) indicated that prior to the first 1960 debate, Nixon's production advisor "objected strenuously" to the use of reaction shots whereas Kennedy's advisors wanted more of them. Further, they continued to press director Don Hewitt on this issue during the debates. The results of the first debate seemed to confirm the expectations of both camps. Seltz and Yoakam observed, "In reaction shots Nixon's eyes darted around, perspiration was clearly noticeable on his chin, and with the tight shots used by Hewitt these things were more obvious" (1977, p. 95). The pressure on this issue continued during the remaining debates, resulting in strict adherence by network directors to equal time with regard to the number and length of reaction shots.

Research on the 1976 Ford and Carter debates suggests that reaction shots do make a difference. Frye and Bryski (1978) reported that Carter was shown reacting to Ford more often, and that Carter projected a positive image and Ford a negative image in reaction shots. Tiemens (1978) concurred, indicating that Carter exhibited more positive facial expression than Ford in reaction shots.

The use of reaction shots acknowledges that there are two or more candidates, and that debates are confrontations between the candidates. Hence, those who stage debates support the use of reaction shots as a way to enhance the confrontational nature of the events. As Hewitt observed, "I tried to put myself in the position of the viewer, and there were certain times when if the guy at home had been in the studio, I'm sure he would have looked over to see what Kennedy's reaction was to what Nixon was saying, and vice versa" (Seltz & Yoakam, 1977, p. 89).

Studies indicate that the use of reaction shots do support the image of confrontation. For example, a study by Messaris, Eckman, and Gumpert of the 1976 debates found that the camera treatment exaggerated the confrontational impression of the debates through "an overemphasis on the extent to which the candidates were interacting with each other"

(1979, p. 361). By 1980 things had changed, and Tiemens, Hellweg, Kipper, and Phillips (1985) indicated that the minimal confrontation evident was reduced even further in the camera treatment that showed the two candidates looking at their counterparts only three times.

Morello's insightful examination of 1984 Reagan and Mondale debates provides further evidence on the relationship between camera treatment and actual and perceived confrontation. Morello concluded that the camera treatment in the two debates, by misusing "close-ups of" or "two-shots with" an opponent (the camera techniques employed to depict reaction), had the effect of misrepresenting the verbal clash (1988a, p. 280). First, by not employing sufficient close-ups or two-shots, they ignored instances of clash. Second, by maintaining consistent and limited use of close-ups and two-shots, they distorted the amount of clash. And third, by the seemingly arbitrary use of reaction shots they distorted which candidate initiated the most clash.

Finally, the pacing of the visual images in debates is an issue that involves camera treatment. More camera shot variety can be employed by directors to increase the perceived pace of debates. One study (cited in Drucker, 1989) reported the use of this technique during the 1984 debates. Another study found that the visual pace quickened for a candidate who "scored in a vital exchange," and that the faster pace "may interfere with audience comprehension of verbal messages" (Morello, 1988b, p. 240).

Candidate Strategies and Visual Image

Once negotiations over format and procedure are completed—Kraus (1988) indicated that they can be quite intense—most decisions on staging and production shift beyond the direct control of the candidates or their advisors. Still, candidates can employ a number of communication techniques in televised debates to enhance their visual images. Martel (1983) called these techniques "physical tactics," and the evidence previously culled indicates that they do make a significant difference in candidate image in televised debates.

Martel claimed that the candidate who takes the stage last can "heighten his command of the stage," particularly if coupled with the offer of a handshake to the opponent, as Ronald Reagan did in his 1980 debate with Jimmy Carter. "Not only did the handshake project Reagan's command and friendliness, but it caught Carter noticeably by surprise before at least 100 million viewers" (1983, p. 78).

Eye contact becomes a critical consideration in this era of televised debates because the camera, via the close-up, provides viewers with close, intimate access to candidates' facial cues. Furthermore, the close-up is the staple of most reaction shots, which capture candidates' responses to opponents' verbal attacks.

An important factor in John Kennedy's more attractive image in the 1960 debates was his superior use of eye contact (Berry, 1987; Katz & Feldman, 1977). Martel added, "Kennedy . . . projected maturity and confidence . . . Nixon had eye contact problems throughout the debates; he often shifted his eyes dartingly and awkwardly toward Kennedy without turning to look at him directly" (1983, p. 79). Similarly, Ronald Reagan's image in the 1980 debate was enhanced by his effective use of eye contact (Wingerson, 1982). Martel explains that Reagan's pre-debate preparations stressed eye contact. "He was advised to look at Carter when expressing righteous indignation and . . . was further counseled to avoid looking downward . . . which can suggest lack of confidence, indecisiveness, or lack of preparation." (1983, p. 79).

The smile is a very important tactic in televised debates. Martel maintained that "the smile is a major means by which the candidate can simultaneously project confidence, control, 'the nice guy image,' and even superiority" (1983, p. 83). Rosenberg and McCafferty (1987, p. 37) reported that candidates' occasional smiles make a significant difference in how voters perceive them. Martel claimed that candidate smiles contributed to both Kennedy's and Reagan's successes in televised debates. Henry (1985) argued that the smile was a contributing factor in Walter Mondale's success against Reagan in the first 1984 debate and Geraldine Ferraro's shortcomings against Bush in the 1984 vice-presidential debate.

Martel also advised candidates to dress for televised debates in "well-pressed, attractive, but reasonably conservative business suits, complemented by white or telegenic blue shirts and coordinated ties" (1983, p. 82). Nixon's choice of a gray suit, which blended into the light set background, was thought to have contributed to his image problems in the first 1960 debate (Mickelson, 1989; Seltz & Yoakam, 1977).

TELEVISION NEWS COVERAGE OF PRESIDENTIAL DEBATES

Television news coverage of presidential debates impacts those who viewed the actual debate and those who did not. Jeff Greenfield tersely warned: "Never make the mistake of assuming that once the debate is over, it is over. The real fight is just beginning: the fight to win the interpretation" (1982, p. 215).

Although it is not the purpose of this book to thoroughly examine television news, the story of the visual dimension of presidential debates would be incomplete without dealing with news coverage of presidential debates. The foundation for this treatment was already laid in our discussion of television as a visual medium.

Television's emphasis on visual messages biases its news coverage of presidential debates, undermining their substantive component. The presence of serious time constraints, magnified by an operating imperative to report stories via a combination of verbal and visual content, has resulted in political coverage via sound bite. As Mickelson concluded, "It is almost impossible to find an outlet on commercial television news programs than allows for much more depth than a sound bite provides" (1989, p. 164). Hence, Jamieson's charge, "In this electronic age, they [labels] are our politics" (1988, p. 248), and the findings by researchers that voters get more information about candidates and their positions from their political advertisements than from television news (Greenfield, 1982; Kern, 1989; Patterson & McClure, 1976), make perfect sense.

What does television news emphasize? Most analysts believe that it is the competitive dimension of political campaigns; the question of who is winning and losing; the horse race (Graber, 1980a; Patterson, 1980; Shaw & McCombs, 1977). Why? Because the competitive dimension is more dramatic, conforming more clearly to narrative forms, which are used in most network entertainment (Gregg, 1977; Weaver, 1976). Cleveland (1969, p. 195) maintained that television reporters "are obliged to present much of their material in the context of crude narrative forms which place great emphasis on threats and conflicts." A memorandum to his staff from former NBC News executive producer Reuven Frank read:

Every news story should, without any sacrifice of probity or responsibility display the attributes of fiction, of drama. It should have structure and conflict, problem and denouncement, rising action and falling action, a beginning, a middle, and an end. These are not only the essentials of drama; they are the essentials of narrative. (Gregg, 1977, p. 224)

David Swanson examined television news coverage of the 1976 presidential campaign. He reported that television's preoccupation with considerations of audience share results in a "melodramatic imperative" as the "frame of reference for reporting campaigns" (1977, p. 241). What this means for television news coverage of presidential debates is an emphasis on who wins the debate and its implications for who will win the election. The verbal and visual content of a debate is subservient to, and is ultimately subsumed by, this dominant preoccupation. Chaffee and Dennis reported that in one study "more than half the press coverage was *about* the debates, but not *of* the debates themselves" (1979, p. 84). Swanson commented on the coverage of the 1976 Carter and Ford debates:

Coverage focused not so much on what was said as on a desperate search for who won, hence who now had momentum and could claim the role of hero. The debates were treated "as contests, and thus as part of the larger horse race." . . . It was clear that television news in particular was unable to deal with the substance of the debates and could only discuss them within its melodramatic frame of reference. (1977, p. 246)

Presidential candidates and their handlers, fully aware that television news attempts to name a winner, seek to influence the media's perspective on the debate. Martel referred to this as one facet of "metadebating," or "debate about debates" (1983, p. 150). As Martel described:

Immediately following a debate, a well-organized campaign will have supporters of the candidate ready to express to the media their satisfaction with the candidate's performance and to explain why they thought he won. . . . The metadebate continues in the succeeding days as the candidates and their surrogates interpret the event to the public. This usually takes the form of focusing attention on any unfortunate statements or gaffes by the opposition. (1983, pp. 168–69)

Such tactics have grown so commonplace that they now have a name: spin control. (Those who engage in these practices are dubbed spin doctors.) Following the 1988 Bentsen and Quayle vice-presidential debate, NBC anchor Tom Brokaw commented: "There was so much spinning going on here tonight it's a wonder the Omaha Civic Auditorium didn't lift off into orbit" (Brydon, 1989, p. 1).

One key strategy that has evolved over the years is to win the "expectations game." This means lowering expectations for your side and raising them for your opponent. The goal is to have the press report even a narrow loss for your candidate as a "better than expected performance," and hence a win. Combined with spin control, this strategy involves putting the best slant or spin on your side's debate performance. Thus, after a presidential debate each side has a spin patrol of supporters declaring how well its candidate did. The goal is to influence reporters and hence public perception of their candidate's success. As is discussed in Chapter 5, several surveys (Ferguson, et al.,

1989; Lang & Lang, 1980; and Steeper, 1980) have established the importance of post-debate commentary in affecting public perceptions of debates.

The expectations game was first played in 1960. According to Martel, "In the first 1960 debate, John Kennedy not only outperformed Richard Nixon, but . . . the strength of his performance was at least partially rooted in his ability to overcome expectations, based on his youth and relative inexperience, that he would be no match for the Vice President" (1983, p. 36).

By 1976, the expectations game was a part of the candidates' strategy. Martel noted that ironically

Jimmy Carter was expected to win the first domestic policy debate by attacking Gerald Ford's record, but when Ford acquitted himself well, he was credited with the win. Conversely, Carter, who was not expected to do well in the foreign policy debate, was helped by this audience expectation and by media attention to Ford's East European gaffe. (1983, p. 36)

By the 1980 debates, the politicians had become pros at playing expectations games. Robert Scott pointed out how pre-debate publicity affected post-debate reactions:

In pushing hard to put Reagan on the defensive, Carter fulfilled the prophecy of the press. His efforts looked strategic because they had been so labeled well in advance for instant identification. Reagan's manner, much more than his actual replies, stamped him as a well-prepared, cool adversary, perhaps fitting the role repeatedly polished by the commentators waiting for the debate: being presidential. (1981, p. 32).

Banker discussed the expectations game that preceded the 1984 debates and the spin control that followed them. He noted: "Probably the most noticeable feature of reporters' coverage is that they tend to focus on drama and confrontation" (1985, p. 1). However, "Balancing this need to be dramatic is the need to appear 'objective' to the audience and thus maintain credibility" (1985, p. 2). In terms of the pre-debate manipulations, Mondale's advisers engaged in a strategy of "misdirection—by trying to fool Reagan and his briefers about their debate strategy" (1985, p. 3). Using false leaks, Mondale's team tried to "help ensure that Reagan would be prepared for a fighting Fritz instead of a gentleman Fritz" (1985, p. 4). Reagan's advisers, on the other hand, focused their pre-debate strategy on trying to raise the expectations of reporters as to what would constitute a Mondale victory (1985, p. 5). Banker pointed out that an important element of the pre-debate strategy of both sides was "preparing the candidate to win the 'sound bite battle' and preparing top aides for their 'spin patrol' duties" (1985, pp. 6–7). He noted that "snappy counterpunches seem to be the most likely to make the news the next night. Quick, sharp rebuttals contain the elements of cleverness and conflict, elements that make for good drama on the news" (1985, p. 7).

After the first debate in 1984, Mondale, according to Banker, won "the battle of the sound bite" (1985, p. 9) with his response to Reagan's "There you go again" line. He also pointed out that Reagan's spin doctors failed to convince reporters that he had not lost. Two days after the debate, the *Wall Street Journal* raised the issue of Reagan's age, and that issue echoed throughout network coverage.

Faced with the age issue and a decline in the polls, Reagan hit on the strategy of blaming the advisers. For example, Paul Laxalt was seen on ABC News saying: "We had six dress rehearsals last time, 90 minutes of intensity. Plus loading him with computer stats, briefing books, the man was absolutely smothered by extraneous material. This time we're going to let Ronald Reagan be Ronald Reagan" (Banker, 1985, p. 20). As Banker put it: "This drama was perfectly acted. The explanation for the debate debacle was not Reagan's age." Rather, Laxalt blamed it on the failures of other aides (1985, p. 20).

Banker claimed that "Mondale's team lacked a coherent plan to use the media for the second debate" (1985, p. 22) and that it was Reagan who won the sound bite war. "Reagan was to win this battle by getting off the memorable line in the debate, a joke about age that helped to deflate the issue. . . . This was shown on all three networks the next night" (1985, p. 24). Thus, after the debate, "it would be the Mondale spin patrol that had the harder task" (1985, p. 25).

The 1988 debates again featured the expectations game and spin control. Herbeck pointed out that "Bush's campaign intentionally attempted to create low expectations for the Vice President" (1989, p. 5). However, Dukakis did not seek to lower his expectations. Carlin discussed the phenomenon of spin control, which "is intended to influence viewers' perceptions of what they saw and heard. It is also intended to shape media reports of the debates. . . . For those who did not view or hear the debates, spin control and media interpretations can become the whole debate" (1989, pp. 210–11).

One attempt to place the expectations game in the context of traditional argumentation was presented by Brydon who wrote:

The presumption in favor of the status quo never really shifted throughout the debate period. Going into the series of debates, people were by and large satisfied with the way the country was going. To the extent that there was any risk associated with George Bush's candidacy, it was associated with his choice of Dan Quayle as his vice-presidential nominee. By lowering Quayle's expectations to almost nothing, the overwhelming victory of Bentsen over Quayle was blunted. (1990b, p. 23)

Brydon (1989) also examined how the three major television networks covered the post-debate spin of the 1988 presidential and vice-presidential debates. Although network correspondents were the most frequent speakers, partisans and candidate representatives initially received significant air time, but were banished from two of the three networks by the final debate. Networks constructed the debates primarily as sporting contests and television performances. Only CBS devoted significant attention to the debates as a clear clash over issues.

This review suggests that, with time, candidates have become more and more concerned with the pre-debate expectations game and the post-debate spin control. This has clearly impacted the verbal content of their debates, as they seek to construct memorable sound bites and influence the character of post-debate commentary by the networks. Banker asserted: "For voters, a presidential campaign resembles a carnival's hall of mirrors. What we see depends on what is reflected in news coverage, and both reporters and candidates are fighting over what it will be" (1985, p. 27). Greenfield supported this point in saying, "Many people watching the debates will not know what they have seen until the next day notices tell them" (1982, p. 215).

Five studies assessed viewer perceptions of who won debates by using two groups: one isolated from, the other exposed to, the network's post-debate commentary. Lang and Lang's (1984) study of the first 1976 Carter and Ford debate found that those who were sampled immediately after the debate thought Carter had done the better job of debating by nearly a two-to-one margin. By contrast, viewers who were exposed to post-debate commentary and then were sampled thought Ford had done the better job by nearly a two-to-one margin. "Here Ford led Carter by roughly the same margin as Carter had previously led Ford" (1984, p. 181).

Frederick Steeper (1980) employed a panel of Seattle voters whereas Patterson (1980) relied on national survey data to gauge public reaction to the second 1976 Carter and Ford debate that contained Ford's gaffe on Eastern Europe. Steeper reported "a huge 51 percent change between late Wednesday and Thursday nights in the voters' perceptions of who had done the 'better' job in the debate," favoring Carter (1980, p. 85).

Patterson found a 47 percent shift between those interviewed less than twelve hours after the debate and those interviewed between twelve and forty-eight hours after the debate, also favoring Carter (1980, p. 123). Patterson concluded, "On their own, voters failed to see in his remark the significance that the press would later attach to it" (1980, p. 125).

Finally, Ferguson, Hollander, and Melwani (1989) and Lemert, Rosenberg, Elliott, Bernstein, and Nestvold (1989) examined the 1988 Bentsen and Quayle vice-presidential debate, identifying a significant difference in the perceptions of viewers about which candidate did the better job of debating between those isolated from and those exposed to post-debate commentary. The latter conclude: "Respondents' reactions to Quayle were not as harsh immediately after the debate as they were later" (Lemert et al., 1989, p. 14).

We examine the effects of presidential debates in some detail in Chapter 5. What is important to note at this time is that television news, because it views presidential debates as contests, tends to focus its coverage of debates on the verbal and visual content that supports claims about which candidate won or lost. That content more often than not consists of "one, dramatic incident which stands out as distinct from all of the words and actions of the candidates" (Morello, 1980, p. 3), such as Ford's gaffe about Eastern Europe in 1976, Reagan's "There you go again" quip in 1980, Reagan's clever comment on "my opponent's youth and inexperience" in 1984, and Bentsen's "Senator, you're no Jack Kennedy" line in 1988. Television news commentary does influence viewers' perceptions about debates, as research shows. As Blankenship and Kang explained, "The way reporters talk about (construct) the debates *have* played an important role in public perception of 'what happened' " (1991, p. 308).

Chapter Five

The Impacts of Presidential Debates

Very likely the debates may only reinforce an opinion already held, or create uncertainties that finally are resolved in terms of surface impressions or party affiliation. But they can have, undeniably, a major, if not decisive, influence.

—Columnists Jack Germond and Jules Witcover
(1979, p. 198)

All research points in one direction: debates have not directly and immediately led to any significant number of changes in voting intentions. Yet, a strong case can be made that, without the televised debates in 1960 and 1980, neither Kennedy nor Reagan would have been elected: the course of history would have been changed.

—Communication Professor Gladys Engel Lang
(1987, p. 211)

Televised presidential debates are among the most watched programs ever broadcast. Approximately 80 percent of Americans viewed at least one debate in 1960 (Katz & Feldman, 1977); 90 percent watched at least one in 1976 (Alexander & Margolis, 1980). As a result, past televised presidential debates have been able to reach in excess of 100 million people (Drucker & Hunold, 1987; Hershey, 1989; Twentieth Century Fund Task Force on Presidential Debates, 1979), far surpassing the typical audience share for all but a handful of televised events.

The important questions are: Do they make any difference? If so, which specific impacts do they generate? The opening quotations to this chapter epitomize the contradictions involving the effects issue. A plethora of scholars have addressed these questions since the advent of televised presidential debates in 1960, often with conflicting results. This chapter delineates the impacts of televised presidential debates, attempting to make some sense out of the maze of seemingly contradictory findings. We examine the effect of past televised presidential debates on the political agenda, socialization, viewer learning about the candidates and their positions, and viewer attitudes and voting disposition.

As indicated previously, we view contemporary presidential debates as unique communication phenomena precisely because they are televised events. This perspective on presidential debates was developed in Chapter 4. Unfortunately, most of the research on debate effects has focused on the impact of what candidates have said in debates, ignoring the unique channel features of television, the medium that carries the content to receivers (Kraus, 1988). Thus, the research that we examine in this chapter may not capture completely the nature, scope, or depth of presidential debate effects (Pfau & Kang, 1989; Wingerson, 1982).

PRESIDENTIAL DEBATES AND THE POLITICAL AGENDA

The political agenda involves a perception of those things that are important. Walter Lippmann (1922) first posited that the mass media help determine people's agendas, particularly about the "unseen environment," where the mass media provides the only contact with reality. Although the political agenda has a number of dimensions, two of the more important elements involve evaluative cues used to assess the strengths and weaknesses of candidates, as well as the relative salience of political issues. The question remains as to whether the content raised by the journalists or the candidates during debates, or the post-debate analysis of that content or of candidates' performance, exerts an impact on the political agenda. The available research on this question indicates mixed results.

Katz and Feldman's synthesis of research on the effects of the 1960 Kennedy-Nixon debates identified a modest agenda impact. They point to a study by Richard Carter of approximately one hundred residents in and around Stanford, California, and a national poll conducted by Opinion Research Corporation concluding: "The debates made some issues more salient," including Quemoy and Matsu, U.S. prestige abroad, unemployment, social security, and education (1977, p. 202).

However, research on the 1976 Carter-Ford debates is less supportive of an agenda impact. Swanson and Swanson combined a content analysis of the first Carter-Ford debate with an experimental assessment of the impact of the debate on eighty-three University of Illinois undergraduate students. They reported that "the first debate had an important effect on voters" as viewers melded their issue priorities and the issues covered during the debate, "showing an agenda-setting effect" (1978, p. 353). On the other hand, research by Jack McLeod, Jean Durall, Dean Ziemke, and Carl Bybee (1979) and Becker, Weaver, Graber, and McCombs (1979) reported no agenda effect of the debates, while a synthesis of all 1976 studies by Sears and Chaffee concluded, "The debates did not set any new agenda," but they did foster crystallization of the differences between candidates on many issues (1979, p. 237). It seems fair to conclude, as did Becker, Weaver, Graber, and McCombs, that the main reason for the absence of an agenda effect is that the political agendas of most voters are established gradually over an entire political season (starting with the first primaries) (1979, p. 427). The 1976 Carter-Ford debates took place too late in the campaign to change them.

A study by Brydon of the effects of the 1984 Reagan-Mondale debates concluded that, as a result of Reagan's poor performance in the first debate, the question of Reagan's age temporarily surfaced as the "number one topic." Thus, Brydon concludes: "Perhaps the major impact of the first debate was its agenda-setting function" (1985a, p. 18).

Thus, some studies indicate a modest political agenda and others find no such effect. However, Becker, Weaver, Graber, and McCombs' explanation of their 1976 null findings (1979) suggests that debates which raise entirely new candidate qualification or issue content, or that occur late in a contest that features a large number of undecided voters, or debates that occur early in a campaign for party nomination, may exert a sizable impact on the political agenda. This possibility is consistent with recent research indicating that mass media content agenda interacts with other variables (e.g., the receiver's need for information) in impacting political agendas (Kaid & Sanders, 1985; O'Keefe & Atwood, 1981). The effect of presidential debates on the political agenda, controlling for the political context, has not been examined to date.

THE ROLE OF PRESIDENTIAL DEBATES IN SOCIALIZATION

In describing the development of people's attitudes about political parties, the authors of *The American Voter* noted, "An orientation toward political affairs typically begins before the individual attains voting age and . . . this orientation strongly reflects his immediate social milieu, in particular, his family" (Campbell, Converse, Miller & Stokes, 1960, pp. 146–47). Hyman terms the process of acquiring political attitudes as "political socialization," and identifies the family as the most powerful source of influence during this process (Hyman, 1959).

Do presidential debates affect political socialization? The limited data suggest that televised presidential debates, because they stimulate young people's awareness of, and interest in, the political process, promote discussion about these matters within families and thus contribute to political socialization. A study by Becker, Pepper, Wenner, and Kim (1979) reports that the 1976 Carter and Ford debates "stimulated political talk" with friends and family members.

While debates foster family interaction about politics, the political attitudes of parents exert considerable influence on young people's attitudes about candidate preference. Desmond and Donohue (1981) examined 156 junior high school students to assess what influenced their perceptions of the first 1976 presidential debate. They reported that debate viewing increased the level of family communication about Carter and Ford and their positions, and that parental comments about who won the debate exerted a substantial influence on their children. James Anderson and Robert Avery (1978) administered tests to families in each of five locations immediately after each of the 1976 Carter-Ford debates. The results demonstrated that the family provides a firm anchor for voting preferences. Anderson and Avery found that family factors are more influential than the debates in changing family member preferences, but that debates exert influence on family members' perceptions of their own and of candidates' positions.

Finally, a study by Hawkins, Pingree, Smith, and Bechtolt (1979) examined the effects of debate viewing on 561 students in the sixth, ninth, and twelfth grades. Debate viewing appeared to assist the sixth- and ninth-grade students in tying together their candidate preferences, their party preferences, and their perceptions of candidate images. Further, bonding of candidate preference and candidate issue positions was strengthened through debate viewing, but only for twelfth-grade students. Hawkins, Pingree, Smith, and Bechtolt (1979) concluded that presidential debate viewing can have significant, direct impact on adolescent political socialization.

IMPACT OF PRESIDENTIAL DEBATES ON LEARNING

Existing knowledge about televised presidential debates and candidate and issue learning is based almost exclusively on the various studies of interparty exchanges involving major party nominees during the general election phase of the 1960, 1976, and 1980 presidential campaigns. Virtually all studies concur that presidential debates increase the manifest information available to the public. Kraus summarizes this body of research:

Scanning the data from at least three presidential elections in which televised debates were held . . . the evidence is clear: (1) candidates discuss a variety of issues; (2) more often than not, candidates can be set apart by the issues; (3) voters learn about issues; (4) candidate issue positions are clarified; (5) some issues become more salient than others; and (6) voters remember the content of debates, especially as it relates to their own lives. (1988, p. 122)

Scholars disagree, however, on the amount of learning that takes place; they disagree considerably on whether learning makes any difference in candidate preference.

Before examining specific studies on debate learning, we pass along Graber's insightful caveat about studies that purport to assess the impact of presidential debates on viewer learning and/or influence. Graber cautioned that many of these studies suffer from one or more methodological shortcomings, termed "treacherous reefs that have not yet been adequately marked by buoys" (1980b, p. 105). Such shortcomings include difficulties involved in isolating debate effects from broader campaign effects; sensitization of subjects; use of crude and distinct measures of learning; and ambiguities and biases in question wording and interpretation.

Viewers Learn Less Than Expected

Viewer expectations for presidential debates are high, and debates typically fall short in comparison. One study employed the uses and gratifications theory, which maintains that people use the mass media for specific purposes such as learning or escape. It compared viewer expectations and learning, by paneling Akron, Ohio, voters before and after the first 1976 Carter-Ford debate. Before the debate, Garrett O'Keefe and Harold Mendelsohn found lofty expectations. Almost 90 percent of their subjects anticipated that the debate would provide more information about the candidates and their positions (1979, p. 409). When the dust settled following the debate, however, only about a fourth of viewers "reported deriving such information from the first debate" (1979, p. 410). Another study, employing a small panel of Midwestern and New England potential voters, reported viewer disappointment with the format of the 1976 debates and "modest learning" (Graber & Kim, 1978).

Other research concurs that presidential debates contribute very little to viewer learning about issues. Bishop, Oldendick, and Tuchfarber report that the first 1976 Carter-Ford debate failed "to boost the contribution of issues to the voters' calculus relative to the weight of party identification" among their Cincinnati, Ohio, subjects (1980, p. 106). They found that party remained the dominant factor in viewer perception; that "voters lack the knowledge and motivation to deal with" the intricacies of contemporary issues; and that debate viewing contributes to a "growing information gap" between receivers who already are more informed versus those less informed about candidates and their positions (1980, p. 196).

Rose (1979) reported the findings of a series of research efforts in conjunction with the Center for Political Studies 1976 American National Election study. These findings indicate that viewers learned about the candidates and their positions, but that learning did not facilitate viewer discrimination between candidates or significantly impact voting intentions. Further, Rose indicates that some learning was unfavorable to candidates, particularly regarding Ford who was the incumbent. In a study of the informational role of the 1976 debates, Hagner and Rieselbach (1980) reported that, since viewers' political party affiliation, candidate preference, and candidate image perception exert the strongest impact on viewer evaluations of candidates' debate performances, the 1976 debates offered little in the way of new political information.

A number of studies focused primarily on candidate images. Bowes and Strentz (1979) examined the process of image formation and change, specifically as it relates to candidate attribute and issue stereotyping. The authors zeroed in on four components of stereotyping: (1) polarization, (2) fixedness, (3) reification, and (4) homogenization. A fifth variable, issue congruity, was also incorporated in the analysis. On questioning a two hundred–member panel on four occasions about their reactions to the debates, the researchers concluded that polarization and reification explained the greatest amount of variance for candidate images, and that candidate attributes, and not issues, contributed more to these stereotyping effects.

Debates Enhance Manifest Information

In contrast to the previous studies that indicate modest learning, most studies suggest debate viewing contributes to considerable learning about the candidates and their positions. Richard Carter assessed learning following each of the 1960 Kennedy-Nixon debates (Katz & Feldman, 1977). His findings reveal that 27 percent of viewers felt they had learned about the candidates and the issues, and that "some of what was said was remembered," thus discounting the impact of selectivity in debate viewing. In addition, three studies (Ellsworth, 1965; Kelley, 1960, 1962) found that political debates promote more emphasis on issues than candidate speeches or paid political commercials.

The overwhelming proportion of studies of the 1976 Carter and Ford debates support a significant learning effect. O'Keefe and Mendelsohn's (1979) investigation of Akron, Ohio, voters indicated that many viewers felt they had learned something "new and important" from watching the debates. The Institute for Social Research at the University of Michigan reported that the 1976 presidential debates "were used more than any other medium, including newspapers and magazines, as a source of information about campaign issues" (Twentieth Century Fund Task Force on Televised Presidential Debates, 1979, p. 46).

Miller and MacKuen found that debate viewing in 1976 increased the level of manifest information that members of the public had about the candidates, regardless of their education, political involvement, or general information-seeking habits. The authors also note that this information focused more heavily on candidate attributes such as competence, performance, and personality, than on issues. The learning effect seemed to be linear in that "the more debates that were watched, the more information the respondent had about the candidates" (1979, pp. 276–77). Miller and MacKuen also observed the timeliness of this information in relation to the election.

Other research on the 1976 Carter-Ford debates has demonstrated significant learning effects. A panel study of Wisconsin voters using telephone interviews revealed substantial viewer learning. Chaffee (1978, p. 335) observed that learning occurred "in waves" following each debate, such that the proportion of "don't know" responses dropped significantly following each debate, with the sharpest declines involving those issues covered in the debates. These results are similar to those reported by the Institute of Social Research at the University of Michigan; researchers found that "knowledge about the candidates increased with each succeeding debate" (Twentieth Century Fund Task Force on Televised Presidential Debates, 1979, p. 46). In further analysis of the Wisconsin data, Dennis, Chaffee, and Choe indicated that debates are most useful to issue-oriented voters. They concluded that debate exposure led to a bonding of the vote with candidate issue differences: "Candidate debates function as a *catalyst*. . . . They add information to the environment in which the bonding of other elements takes place. This modification of the environment makes it more likely that issue content will become more closely bonded to the vote" (1979, p. 328).

Other studies also support that the 1976 Carter-Ford debates contributed to a more informed electorate. A national survey by Morrison, Steeper, and Greendale reported that the first 1976 debate resulted in "significant changes in public knowledge of where the candidates stood on certain leading issues" (Chaffee & Dennis, 1979, p. 88). Lupfer and Wald (1979) also examined learning effects of the first Carter-Ford debate. This study demonstrated that the debate was informative, making viewers more aware of specific candidate's positions.

In a survey of Virgina voters, Abramowitz (1978) reported that the first 1976 Carter-Ford debate contributed to "a better-informed electorate," with notable increases in awareness of the candidates' positions on the unemployment issue (1978, p. 689). However, the study indicated that viewer learning did not carry over to candidate preference. "Instead of choosing a candidate in accordance with their issue position, voters chose an issue position in accordance with their candidate preference" (1978, p. 688). In another study, this one involving "five waves" of interviews with thirteen hundred potential voters from upstate New York before the first debate and then after each of the three presidential debates and the one vice-presidential debate, Becker, Sobowale, Cobbey, and Eyal (1980) concluded that a better-informed electorate resulted from viewing the 1976 debates. The authors reported that viewers became more informed about the campaign issues, background and characteristics of the candidates, and ideological aspects of the campaign.

Finally, Sears and Chaffee's (1979) synthesis of studies of the 1976 Carter-Ford debates indicated that "the debates to some degree met the expectation that voters would learn where the candidates stood" (p. 237). The first 1976 debate in particular clearly contributed to viewer learning about the candidates and their positions. Otherwise the debates served mainly to clarify differences between the candidates for viewers (Sears & Chaffee, 1979).

Political Context Sets Learning Parameters

As Graber (1980b) cautioned at the outset of this discussion of presidential debates and learning, it is impossible to isolate debates from the broader political environment. As a result, all attempts to generalize about the impact of televised debates on viewer learning are limited to

Thus: a) debates are more issue-driven than other campaign comm

b) voters do learn something

specific contexts. The truth of the matter is that under some circumstances presidential debates generate substantial character *and* issue learning; in other instances, they produce sizable character *or* issue learning; and in other contexts, they result in minimal learning.

The impact of character and issue concerns varies from one election campaign to another, and even varies over the course of a single campaign. Character, which deals with the attributes of candidates (e.g., their competence, character, warmth, leadership potential, etc.), plays a more decisive role than issues in voter candidate choice criteria (Asher, 1980; Campbell, 1983; DeVries & Tarrance, 1972; Graber, 1980a; Hahn & Goncher, 1972; Kirkpatrick, Lyons & Fitzgerald, 1975; O'Keefe, 1975; Pomper, 1975; Shapiro, 1969). As Chapter 4 indicated, because television places a higher premium on presentational elements, it bears responsibility for the ascendancy of character as the dominant criterion for assessing communicators (Adams, 1983; Graber, 1976; Keating & Latane, 1976; Keeter, 1987; Meyrowitz, 1985; Pfau, 1990; Rudd, 1986).

However, the primacy of character is not constant across a political campaign. Character is important because it is often the first judgment that voters make about candidates. We tend to judge candidates as people before we turn our attention to their specific stands on issues. This also turns out to be a fairly efficient decision standard because it is easier to learn about candidate character than about candidate issue positions (Page, 1978; Weaver, Graber, McCombs & Eyal, 1981). Televised debates and all other campaign communication exerts maximum possible impact on voter learning about candidate character during this formative period when voter perceptions of candidate character are more volatile (Becker & McCombs, 1978; Gopoian, 1982; Kennamer & Chaffee, 1982; Mendelsohn & O'Keefe, 1976; Trent & Friedenberg, 1983; Williams, Weber, Haaland, Mueller & Craig, 1976).

Once voter judgments of candidate character take, the potential of debates or other communication to generate much learning about candidate character diminishes. Indeed, studies document the reduced influence of character messages relative to issue messages on voter attitudes and voting disposition during later stages of campaigns (Hofstetter, Zukin & Buss, 1978; Kinder, 1978; Patterson, 1980; Patterson & McClure, 1976; Pfau & Burgoon, 1989; Pfau, Kenski, Nitz & Sorenson, 1989; Strouse, 1975).

Thus, the prevailing political context determines the role and impact of character and/or issue information on cognitions (Pierce & Sullivan, 1980). J. David Kennamer and Steven Chaffee explain, "The campaign progresses in a series of phases, and the role of the media is quite different, in kind as well as in magnitude, in these successive periods. The character of the audience that is being addressed changes, as does the structure of political information held by the audience" (1982, p. 627).

The political context sets learning parameters. If voters are unsure about the character and/or positions of presidential candidates, either because they are uninformed or because they are conflicted, the potential of televised presidential debates to promote viewer learning is great. This window of opportunity for debate learning varies from election to election.

In their study of the influence of mass media news during early presidential primaries, Kennamer and Chaffee point to the early nomination phase as particularly ripe for potential learning. "What appears clear . . . is that the very early phase is characterized by widespread lack of information among those who are not following the campaign closely, and uncertainty even among those who are" (1982, p. 647).

Thus, televised intraparty debates during the presidential selection process carry real potential to inform viewers about candidate character and positions because they take place early in a campaign before the initial formation of viewer perceptions (e.g., Jimmy Carter in 1976, George Bush in 1980, Gary Hart in 1984, Michael Dukakis in 1988), or in other cases, prior to the solidification of viewer perceptions (e.g., Ronald Reagan in 1980, Walter Mondale in 1984, George Bush in 1988).

The research on the impact of intraparty debates on viewer learning is limited. One study of the second Republican debate in 1980, broadcast nationally on public television and featuring all seven declared candidates, found that debate viewing made a significant contribution to viewers' knowledge of, and subsequent interest in, the campaign (Lemert, Elliott, Nestvold & Rarick, 1983). A second study of three 1984 Democratic primary debates affirmed that intraparty debates generate "substantial learning" (Pfau, 1988). The findings indicated that each of the debates produced significant viewer learning regarding each candidate, about most issues, and among all categories of viewers.

The potential of televised presidential debates that take place during general election campaigns to affect viewer learning depends largely on the political context in which they occur. Debates during election contests featuring more uninformed and/or conflicted voters, for whom information holds greater utility, generate more learning (Chaffee & Choe, 1980; Geer, 1987). However, this question requires further study.

Nonetheless, one thing is clear. To the extent that people who are uninformed later in a presidential campaign are also likely to be less motivated, televised debates fuel an information gap between more informed and less informed. Roberts's study of media use during the 1976 presidential campaign makes just this point. "Instead of seeking help from respected sources of communication such as televised debates, those who report difficulty [less informed and less motivated people] are more likely to turn to briefer forms of political communication such as television advertisements as an aid in decision-making" (1979, p. 802). Roberts's explanation makes sense of Graber and Kim's (1978) finding that televised debates offer more knowledge to the most knowledgeable, and of Bishop, Oldendick, and Tuchfarber's (1978) conclusion that watching presidential debates widens the existing information gap between the "knowledge-rich" and the "knowledge-poor."

PERSUASIVE IMPACT OF PRESIDENTIAL DEBATES

Much discord in political communication has centered on the question as to whether or not political debates produce changes in viewer attitudes toward candidates, thus influencing voting. The dominant theoretical views at the time of the Kennedy-Nixon encounters were that political debates and other campaign communication do not significantly impact candidate selection. Nonetheless, some scholars detected influence. A different view emerged by the seventies based on the notion that while political debates and other campaign communication possess the potential for sizable influence, their impact varies based on receivers' attitude predisposition, largely a function of the prevailing campaign context.

Do televised presidential debates produce changes in viewer attitudes toward candidates, thus influencing voting? A morass of contradictions plague extant research findings. Some studies support, and others fail to support, the influence of televised presidential debates on viewer attitudes toward candidates. The two opening quotations by Germond and Witcover (1979) and Lang (1987) epitomize the lack of consensus about televised presidential debate influence. Furthermore, because the search for effects peaked with the 1976 debates, we are forced to rely more and more heavily on survey research to deduce the probable effects of the 1980, 1984, and 1988 debates.

Persuasive Impact of the 1960 Debates

Most assessments of the impact of the 1960 Kennedy and Nixon debates were grounded in the gestalt of that era: a pessimistic view of the typical voter as largely inactive and uninterested when it came to political matters, unable and/or unwilling to identify and evaluate issue appeals, and inclined to vote according to party identification (Campbell, Converse, Miller & Stokes, 1960; Campbell, Gurin & Miller, 1954; Hyman, 1959), and a limited effects perspective of mass media communication based on the persuasive impotence of mass media political appeals (Berelson, Lazarsfeld & McPhee, 1954; Katz & Lazarsfeld, 1955; Lazarsfeld, Berelson & Gaudet, 1968).

Given such theoretical assumptions, one might expect that studies of the effects of the 1960 Kennedy-Nixon debates would conclude that the debates produced only a small impact on the election outcome. Indeed, this was the conclusion of most studies.

Samuel Lubell's (1977) interviews with prospective voters during the 1960 campaign led him to the conclusion that while the Kennedy-Nixon debates strengthened Kennedy's image, they did not appreciably affect voting disposition. Similarly, Lang and Lang's examination of New York City viewers found that the debates resulted in "some rather dramatic changes in candidate image" favoring Kennedy, but only small changes in voting intentions (1977, p. 328). Sebald (1962) reported that the 1960 debates largely reinforced attitude predispositions. He concluded that through selective attention, perception, and recall viewers were drawn to images and information that supported the candidate of the preferred party, missing content opposed to that candidate.

Katz and Feldman (1977) examined 31 studies of the debates and, in assessing the impact of the debates on the election outcome, concluded that while the first debate shifted attitudes toward Kennedy, the debates mainly strengthened viewer attitudes toward their preferred candidate and party. The authors concede, however, that this crystallization of attitudes worked more to Kennedy's advantage, and that overall the 1960 debates may have produced a slight shift in voting disposition toward Kennedy (1977, pp. 209, 211–12).

Nonetheless, some data suggested that the Kennedy-Nixon debates produced substantial impact. Ben-Zeev and White (1977) reported that especially for undecided voters, the debates shifted public opinion toward Kennedy, and that the average gain for Kennedy was four percentage points per debate. Middleton (1962) found that the debates played "an extremely important role" in the voting decision process for one out of every eight registered voters in his Tallahassee, Florida, sample.

Rosenthal (1963) concluded that Kennedy's personality, his perceived intelligence and sincerity, resulted in a significant, positive persuasive effect. Tannenbaum, Greenberg, and Silverman (1977) examined perceptions of candidate images before, during, and after the 1960 debates among female college students. They concluded that the first debate served as a catalyst to changes in the viewer images of the two candidates, such that Kennedy's image became more favorable, and Nixon's less favorable, as the debates progressed. In short, a number of studies indicate that the 1960 debates produced more positive attitudes toward Kennedy. Did these attitudes translate into votes? Pollster Elmo Roper (1960, pp. 10–13) estimated that four million voters changed their voting intent as a result of the debates.

Persuasive Impact of the 1976 Debates

Rival assumptions about the electorate and mass media communication surfaced between 1960 and 1976. These perspectives held that the electorate is more ideological, thus more likely to utilize issue content in assessing political candidates and less inclined to vote a straight party position (Axelrod, 1972; Boyd, 1972; Brody & Page, 1972; DeVries & Tarrance, 1972; Miller & Levitan, 1976; Nie & Anderson, 1976; Nie, Verba & Petrocik, 1976; Pomper, 1972, 1975; Repass, 1971; Shapiro, 1969; Weisberg & Rusk, 1970), and that mass media communication involves an active receiver so that in certain circumstances, communication via the mass media can achieve significant persuasive results (Blumler & McQuail, 1969; McQuail, Blumler & Brown, 1972; Sheingold, 1973). Given the competition among old and new theoretical assumptions, it is not surprising that research findings were mixed regarding the impact of the 1976 Carter-Ford debates.

Some studies on the Carter-Ford debates reported small or moderate effects. Sanders, Kimsey, and Hantz (1977) conducted a three-stage panel study. Results of their interviews with 1,927 subjects indicated that viewers were generally disappointed with the debates. In addition, the authors found that the debates did not significantly alter viewer voting preferences. Wald and Lupfer (1978) examined the attitudes of viewers and nonviewers at three points: one week before the first debate; immediately after the first debate; and one week following the first debate. The results indicated that the first debate exerted no significant effect on viewer voting intention.

Cundy and Havick (1977) reported a strong selectivity effect from viewing the 1976 debates. They found that 82.2 percent of the Carter supporters and 93.5 percent of the Ford supporters voting as they would have absent debates. Further, their biases colored judgments of the candidates' personalities, positions, and performance in the debates. Debate viewing exerted a greater impact on independents who experienced much less selectivity than partisans. Similarly, in examining data gathered by the Center for Political Studies at the University of Michigan, Feigert and Bowling (1980) reported that the debates primarily reinforced voting decisions of viewers with a prior candidate preference, and even exerted minimal impact on the voting intention of those without a prior preference. In discussing the results of survey research, Lesher, Caddell, and Rafshoon (1979) concluded that the debates served primarily to reinforce the voting decisions of those who had a firm preference between the candidates.

Mulder (1978) conducted a study of the first 1976 debate using telephone interviews before and after the debate. Results indicated that the debates increased interest in the campaign but did not work to the competitive advantage of either candidate. Interestingly, Mulder found that viewers lost confidence in both candidates as a result of watching the debate. Eadie, Krivonos, and Goodman (1977) sampled the attitudes of 120 people in five regions of the country after the first 1976 debate. The authors found that the debate produced no overall changes in attitude or candidate preference, although it did solidify support for both candidates.

The reinforcement impact of the debates was revealed in other studies as well. Examining data collected by Indiana University and Knight-Ridder Newspapers at various intervals from late May until the day after the election, Hagner and Rieselbach concluded, "The debate reinforced existing predispositions considerably, but actually changed them very little" (1980, p. 178). Miller and MacKuen (1979) also found that the debates served largely to reinforce partisans. They reported "very little change in candidate assessment that could be attributed to debate exposure." However, they conceded that to the extent the debates reinforced wavering Democrats, they may have helped Jimmy Carter "maintain his Democrat majority and thus win an election that was heavily determined by party loyalty" (p. 291). McLeod, Durall, Ziemke, and Bybee (1979) examined younger and older voters in Madison, Wisconsin. They reported that debate viewing served mainly to preempt slippage of soft Democrats from Carter, thus reinforcing traditional voting patterns.

Davis investigated shifts in issue agreement and attribute perception during the 1976 presidential campaign. He concluded that, although the debates fostered more favorable perceptions of Carter, "neither candidate benefited consistently or substantially from the debates" (1979, p. 345). Simons and Liebowitz employed a semantic differential device to measure shifts in candidate images as a result of the 1976 debates. While the researchers found no major shifts in image, they did report that Ford's "image improved somewhat more than Carter's did over the course of the debates" (1979, p. 404). Similarly, Atkin, Hocking, and McDermott's panel survey of Michigan and Georgia voters reported that the third debate "made a small but positive contribution to affect toward each candidate" (1979, p. 435), but that viewer interpersonal interaction with other viewers mediated the direct impact of the debate.

Abramowitz (1978) examined the impact of the first 1976 debate on Virginia voters, concluding, "The debate had almost no impact on voting intentions. There was almost no net change in support for the two candidates and very little shifting of individual preferences" (1978, p. 688). Similarly, Rose's (1979) synthesis of data provided by the Inter-University Consortium for Political and Social Research indicated that viewing produced minimal impact on voting, perhaps "adding one percent or so to Carter's aggregate vote totals" (1979, p. 217).

Smith (1977) also concluded that the 1976 debates benefited neither candidate, enhancing negative images of both Carter and Ford. For example, Ford's ratings increased on such items as impulsiveness, irresponsibility, and dislikableness and Carter's scores increased on cowardice, amateurishness, and impulsiveness. Finally, a study by Bishop, Oldendick, and Tuchfarber (1980) of the 1976 election campaign found that while debates contributed to "a greater degree of integration or 'consistency' between [the viewer's] positions on various issues and their election day behavior," party variables remain a much more important factor influencing voter decision than political debates.

These findings contrast with studies reporting that the 1976 debates made an important difference in the outcome of the election by altering candidate images. One study identified a time lag in debate effects. Barnett measured attitudes of a twenty-person panel over twelve weeks. He found that the first two debates exerted a significant impact on viewer attitudes about the candidates, but that the full impact of debate viewing was not felt until one to two weeks following the events. He attributed the time lag to one of three factors: "(1) an actual lag in attitude change, (2) the time it takes for information to diffuse through the social system, and (3) the agenda-setting function of the media" (1981, p. 162). Krivonos (1976) found that, while initial reactions to the first Carter and Ford debate were divided along partisan lines, viewer attitudes shifted toward Ford during the week following the debate. Krivonos speculated that media coverage of the debate was responsible for the shift.

Other researchers reported significant changes in attitudes about the candidates. Gregory Casey and Michael Fitzgerald (1977) found that debate viewing produced an appreciable shift in viewer images of candidates. Walker and Peterson (1981) revealed a significant positive relationship between viewer exposure to the 1976 debates and attitude change, particularly among undecided voters. Nimmo and Mansfield reported a significant shift in the image of Walter Mondale following the 1976 vice presidential debate. "Mondale's image . . . was not only positive, it was closer to that of the Ideal President measured in 1976 than any other candidate before or since" (1985, p. 8). In a study of Dutch viewers, deBock (1978) found that the presidential debates helped shape presidential preference, regardless of the political orientation of viewers.

A combination of experimental, survey, and anecdotal data points to a rather decisive role for the debates in the outcome of the 1976 presidential campaign. A panel study of potential voters in Cedar Rapids, Iowa, of the first 1976 debate reveals that 26.9 percent of viewers said that "the debate had some effect on their decision about whom they favored" (after the debate 32.2 percent said the debate influenced their choice of candidates) (Becker, Pepper, Wenner & Kim, 1979, p. 387).

Burns Roper offered persuasive evidence that the second Carter-Ford debate was "a turning point in the dynamics of the election. It caused a reversal of trend, a change in thinking—and as a consequence, the election of a President" (1977, p. 12). Robinson's examination of all 1976 poll results led him to conclude that "While only 2–3 percent of all voters mentioned the debates as their reason for voting, the debates . . . were the most often cited reasons for switching to Ford or Carter during the campaign" (1979, p. 265). Carter did not hesitate in attributing the 1976 reversal in the momentum of public opinion—and his victory—to his debates with Gerald Ford (Alexander & Margolis, 1980).

Most analysts concede that presidential debates do affect the attitudes and candidate preferences of undecided voters, and some contend that the 1976 debates may have tipped the balance in the election because of their impact on undecideds. Chaffee and Choe's Wisconsin study (1980) revealed that 31 percent of voters were undecided in the week prior to the debates. Chaffee concluded that "in elections where large numbers of such voters are present, the heavy flow of information created by the debates can be influential" (1978, p. 330). In the same vein, Davis's study (1979) of Cleveland, Ohio, voters found that the 1976 debates "strongly affected" the perceptions of candidate attributes of late deciders. In a synthesis of studies of the 1976 debates, including his own Wisconsin data, Chaffee concluded:

Prior to the debates, many voters reported that they were undecided, and they looked to the debates for information about the candidates' stands on policy issues. The debates provided issue information, and most voters watched and learned from them. Those who were the most regular viewers changed the most in their voting intentions, were the ones least influenced by predispositional factors, and were the most likely to vote in conformance with policy differences they perceived between themselves and the candidates. (1978, p. 341)

As a result, Davis (1979) concluded that the debates were more likely than other forms of mass communication to change voter perceptions of candidates. Geer's retrospective analysis of *New York Times*/CBS News election survey data collected before and after the 1976 debate revealed that "slightly more than 16 percent of those interviewed altered the intensity of their preference, while 10 percent actually switched their support to the opposing candidate" (1988, p. 490).

Persuasive Impact of the 1980, 1984, and 1988 Debates

The volatile conditions that Chaffee described in 1976 were even more evident prior to the Carter-Reagan debate of 1980. Nonetheless, research findings are mixed in 1980 as well.

Using *New York Times*/CBS News election survey data during the period immediately following the Carter-Reagan debate in 1980, Lee Sigelman and Carol Sigelman (1984) found that 86.2 percent of Carter supporters and 96.1 percent of Reagan supporters thought their respective candidate had won the debate. Not surprisingly, the Sigelmans concluded that debates serve mainly to reinforce existing attitudes of partisan viewers. The Sigelmans examined viewers' candidate preferences and their perceptions of debate winners at the same point in time, thus precluding any clear indication of sequencing, which is essential to the notion of causality.

Leuthold and Valentine (1981) reported a modest persuasive impact of the 1980 debate. They were particularly interested in identifying those critical factors that contribute to viewers' beliefs as to which candidate wins a presidential debate. The authors concluded that a candidate with a substantial lead in the polls is likely to be perceived as the winner of a debate as long as that candidate performs at least as well as the opponent. In addition, assuming that the number of supporters of each of the candidates is about equal, the candidate with the more intense supporters, and the more conservative candidate, is more likely to be perceived as the winner of a debate. Vancil and Pendell's telephone survey (1984) following the 1980 debate discovered that 90.8 percent of respondents did not change their minds about the candidates.

Despite these claims, other data suggests that the 1980 Carter-Reagan debate produced substantial shifts in voter perceptions, favoring Reagan. The circumstances were certainly ripe. In 1980, the proportion of undecided and weakly aligned voters was unusually large. Kelley (1983, pp. 170–71) cites results from the *Times*/CBS News election day survey, the ABC News election day survey, and the Gallup postelection survey, to conclude that the proportion of voters who said that they had decided how to vote during the week prior to election day ranged from 23 to 35 percent of the electorate. This, coupled with the fact that only one debate was held, and that it occurred late in the campaign, set the stage for the Carter-Reagan debate to play a decisive role in the outcome of the election.

Furthermore, some data indicate that it did play a decisive role. All major polls confirmed that Reagan outperformed Carter in the debate, although the margin varied (Brydon, 1985b). Those surveyed in the Harris poll scored the debate 44–26 percent for Reagan (Harris, 1980). Reagan was particularly effective with undecided voters. A CBS poll indicated that undecideds went for Reagan in the debate by a two-to-one margin ("Now a Few," 1980).

There was an unusually large proportion of both undecided and conflicted voters on the eve of the 1980 debate, and the available evidence indicates that Reagan's performance produced impressive gains among both groups. Some 18 percent of those responding to a Gallup election day survey indicated that they had *decided how to vote after watching the Carter and Reagan debate* (Kelley, 1983, p. 171). A study by the Institute for Social Inquiry at the University of Connecticut of that state's voters just before and after the Carter and Reagan debate concluded that the debate "produced an extraordinary shift" in the public's perception—favoring Reagan (Ladd & Ferree, 1981, p. 35). "An ABC poll found that among voters who decided during the week after the debate (one-quarter of the electorate), 22 percent cited the debate as the most important factor" (Brydon, 1985b, p. 149).

It appears that many potential Reagan voters used the 1980 debate "as one (if not *the*) major source of evidence regarding Reagan's fitness for the presidency" (Davis, 1982, p. 491). As a result, Davis's study of the 1980 Carter-Reagan debate found that viewers' intentions to vote for Reagan were affected by their perceptions of Reagan's performance, which enhanced their ratings of Reagan's competence, but that intentions to vote for Carter were not affected by his performance (1982, pp. 490–

91). As Kelley reports, "Reagan's performance in the Carter-Reagan debate made many voters more comfortable at the prospect of a Reagan presidency" (1983, p. 172).

Richard Wirthlin, Reagan's pollster, and Patrick Caddell, Carter's pollster, reported that the debate produced a large and immediate shift away from Carter, toward Reagan. As Swerdlow summarized:

Wirthlin discovered that Reagan had picked up two points and Carter had lost five. Caddell concluded that Reagan's personal rating had improved at least five points, that he had gained eleven points on trustworthiness, and that the notion he "shoots from the hip" had decreased by seventeen points. (1984, p. 19)

Wirthlin concluded, "The debate was one—if not the major—conditioning event that established the foundation for the landslide" (Martel, 1983, p. 28). He supported this claim with polling data that depicted a sharply rising Reagan margin after the Tuesday debate—a lead of six points on Wednesday, seven points on Thursday, nine on Friday, and ten on Saturday. Or, as Austin Ranney posited, "Many observers believed that the Cleveland debate more than anything else converted a narrow and shaky Reagan lead into the 10-percentage-point margin by which he won the election a week later" (1983, p. 27).

Conditions on the eve of the 1984 Reagan and Mondale debates were much less volatile than in 1980, thus the televised debates were much less likely to affect viewer attitudes toward the candidates. Reagan was a popular incumbent president with a sizable lead in the polls, and Walter Mondale, who served as vice president in the Carter administration, was a well-established challenger (Saikowski, 1984). As a result, the undecided voting block never exceeded 20 percent of the electorate ("In the Heat," 1984). Nonetheless, a *Times*/CBS News poll showed that the 1984 debates could determine the voting choice of as many as 25 percent of "likely voters" (Weintraub, 1984).

The role of viewer expectations played an important role in assessing candidate performance in the 1984 debates. One study of the first 1984 debate highlighted the role that expectations play in viewer perceptions of who won. Rouner and Perloff's research involving the attitudes of Cuyahoga County, Ohio, potential voters before and after the first 1984 debate found that those who expected Reagan to win the debate "interpreted his performance to confirm their expectations" (1986, p. 8).

The first 1984 debate pitted Reagan, the great communicator, against Mondale, often stiff and dull in his television demeanor, who in his own words, "never warmed up to the electronic media" (Clendinen, 1984, p. 4A). In the first debate, there is good evidence that both candidates violated viewer expectations. Mondale's performance, perceived as smooth, composed, and warm, constituted a positive violation of expectations, while Reagan's performance, seen as halting and uncertain, constituted a negative violation of expectations. One journalist summed up the comparative images generated by the two candidates in these words:

It was clear as the confrontation went on that it was Reagan, normally the smooth, experienced "great communicator" on television who was most taut last night. Beginning with the first question . . . he [Reagan] frequently paused and groped for words . . . Mondale was . . . more forceful and composed, and delivered both his answers and his set closing remarks without a fluff. (Ferguson, 1984, p. 1)

Pfau (1987) has previously reported that, in presidential debates positive violations of expectations promote persuasion, whereas negative violations inhibit, and may retard, attitude change. Elizabeth Drew makes precisely this point about the first 1984 debate:

The two most important things that affected the outcome of the debate—and, more important, the interpretation of the outcome of the debate—were that both Mondale and Reagan did not match the expectations of them: Mondale made a better impression than people had expected; Reagan made a worse one. (1985, p. 686)

The polls reflected immediate movement toward Mondale. A Harris poll revealed Mondale a 61–19 percent winner, reducing the "confidence gap" by 20 points (Reinsch, 1988, pp. 286–87). Two *Times*/CBS News polls illustrated the impact of news commentary on perceptions of who won. Their first poll, done right after the debate, showed Mondale a 43–34 percent winner, a margin that grew to 66–17 percent by their Tuesday poll (Church, 1984a). Shortly thereafter, candidate preferences began to shift as Republican and Democratic pollsters picked up a five- to six-point shift toward Mondale ("Reagan and the," 1984). A *Times*/CBS News poll revealed that Reagan's lead had been cut in half (Raines, 1984). Church explained the reason for the opinion shift: "Mondale's articulate, forceful performance and Reagan's hesitant one seem to be prompting a second look at both contenders by voters who had decided to tune out the campaign" (1984a, p. 26). Most important for Mondale's prospects for defeating Reagan, "the age issue had got out of the closet and become suddenly salient" (Goldman & Fuller, 1985, p. 319).

Expectations are a two-edged sword, however. As a result of Mondale's strong performance and Reagan's weak showing during the first debate, expectations changed, placing Mondale in a no-win scenario for the second debate. Brydon refers to a "reversal of the 'expectations game' " (1985a, p. 19). Goldman and Fuller (1985) report that Reagan's role as "the underdog" in the second debate was an advantage. Or, as *Newsweek* commented, in the first debate Mondale's success was surprising whereas in the second debate it would have been expected (Brydon, 1985a).

Although Mondale performed well in the second debate, he did not rise to the level of the inflated expectations. Brydon observed: "Part of the explanation of Reagan's 'comeback' in the second debate is that expectations were lower for him and higher for Mondale than in the first debate" (1985a, p. 36). Furthermore, in defusing the age issue, Reagan used the well- rehearsed quip: "I am not going to exploit, for political purposes, my opponent's youth and inexperience" (Magnuson & Church, 1984, p. 22). "As it turned out, this was the most remembered comment of the entire debate" (Reinsch, 1988, p. 289).

Overall, Geer's (1988) look at *Times*/CBS News survey data collected before and after each of the 1984 presidential debates revealed that the 1984 debates caused 14 percent of voters to shift their preference, with 5–6 percent changing from one ticket to the other. He acknowledges that the 1984 debates produced smaller persuasive changes than the 1976 debates, attributing this to more intense voter attitudes about the 1984 candidates, incumbent Reagan and challenger Mondale.

The 1988 Bush-Dukakis debates took a back seat to the attack advertising employed during the campaign. Initiated well in advance of the first debate, Bush's attack messages, in particular, established the character and issue agenda for the 1988 campaign (Farah & Klein, 1989; Gronbeck, 1989; Hershey, 1989; Jamieson, 1989; Pfau & Kenski, 1990; Pfau, Kenski, Nitz & Sorenson, 1989). In this context, the 1988 debates needed to break new ground to produce a persuasive impact, but they did not. Marjorie Hershey (1989, p. 89) reports that the first debate, in particular, offered nothing new to viewers; in the debate both candidates simply followed "long-standing scripts." As a result, although Dukakis was viewed as the winner of the first debate, his victory did not produce much movement in the polls.

The 1988 debates served mainly to reinforce—particularly for Dukakis—images of the candidates established via attack advertising. Two studies, both employing undergraduate students as subjects, affirmed that the debates exerted little persuasive impact. Gregory Payne, James Golden, John Marlier, and Scott Ratzan found that prior attitudes largely determine how viewers respond to debates. They concluded, "Debates constitute more of a confirmatory than a persuasive influence with their potential to induce changes in attitude diminishing as opinions crystallize" (1989, p. 434). Pfau and Kang (1989) report that viewing the first 1988 Bush and Dukakis debate reinforced attitudes of partisan viewers but exerted considerable impact on undecideds.

Political Context Determines Influence Potential

Televised presidential debates do affect viewers' attitudes about candidates, at times sufficient to help shape and/or alter viewers' candidate preference. This impact, however, is largely limited to voters who are uninformed or conflicted. Because the proportion of such viewers depends on the context of an election at a particular point in time, the persuasive force of televised debates varies accordingly. As with learning impacts, the window of opportunity for televised debate influence is determined by the political context. As Becker and Kraus, following an extensive review of the political communication literature, posited: "[Studies] demonstrate . . . that campaign communication... can affect voting decisions rather directly—at least when 'one of the candidates is not well known, many voters are undecided, the contest appears to be a close one, and party allegiances are weak' " (1978, p. 267).

Under specific circumstances, presidential debates exert substantial impact. One circumstance involves debates that take place early in an election campaign, particularly during the nomination process, especially of the party out of power. During this phase attitudes are unformed or instable and mass media influence is potentially greatest (Becker & McCombs, 1978; Gopoian, 1982; Kennamer & Chaffee, 1982; Orren, 1985; Williams, Weber, Haaland, Mueller & Craig, 1976). Kennamer and Chaffee explain that during the "mist-clearing and winnowing phases" the mass media can exert "powerful effects" on cognitions and attitudes (1982, p. 647). Becker and McCombs speculated that "the primary season may be a formative period for many voters—a time when they mold their attitudes" (1978, p. 302). Trent and Friedenberg add that during this period "debates can affect public perception of a candidate's image," including judgments of competence and character (1983, p. 271).

Primary and caucus debates exert considerable influence on the acquisition and development of voter perceptions about the personal characteristics of candidates precisely because they occur early in a political campaign, prior to the development of initial impressions and/or the hardening of perceptions about candidates. Gopoian's review of the *Times*/CBS News primary election exit surveys for twenty 1976 presidential primaries found that "the personal characteristics of the candidates played a critical role in determining the candidate preferences of voters" (1982, p. 544). This makes sense because during the contest for nomination party identification, the most powerful factor in voter decision criteria in the general election, is less potent, thus allowing short-term forces (election specific image or issue considerations) to exert more influence in voter decision making (Gopoian, 1982; Orren, 1985).

Consequently, Trent and Friedenberg (1983) maintain that televised debates are most likely to affect candidate image in those instances in which candidates are not well known. Martel points to two specific examples:

It is doubtful that Jimmy Carter could have risen from a 2 percent recognition factor to win the Democratic nomination without his performance in the 1976 candidate forums. Similarly, John Anderson's campaign might never have gotten off of the ground in 1980 had he not distinguished himself in the Iowa Republican forum. (1983, p. 52)

In gauging the relative impact of the 1984 Democratic primary debates, Orren claimed, "The debates in Illinois, Pennsylvania, and New York affected the outcome in those state primaries" (1985, p. 54). This is consistent with the results of Pfau's (1987) experimental study involving the same three 1984 Democratic primary debates that revealed significant changes in attitudes about the two least-known candidates, Gary Hart and Jesse Jackson. Pfau concluded:

Intraparty debates, because they take place during the selection phase of a campaign when voter attitudes about candidates are more volatile, exert substantial influence on viewer attitudes, particularly with regard to less established candidates. The 1984 intraparty debates influenced viewer attitudes about Hart and Jackson; they produced only a slight change in attitude toward Mondale. (1987, p. 694)

The second circumstance in which presidential debates can exert significant impact involves elections featuring substantial undecided or conflicted voters. Chaffee and Choe (1980) examined the decision patterns of various types of voters, with emphasis on those who make decisions during the campaign. Voters designated as "pre-campaign deciders" and "last- minute deciders" cast their ballots mainly according to party identification. By contrast, voters designated as "campaign deciders" were lower in partisanship and more inclined to pay attention to the campaign and to televised presidential debates.

Thus, Geer maintains that the potential effect of debates grows as the number of undecided and conflicted voters increase. On the one hand,

Geer's research shows that in some elections as many as 60–70 percent of all undecided voters choose one or the other candidate following exposure to a debate (1987, p. 20). Geer added, "Debates also can cause many cross-pressured and weakly committed individuals to change their preference for president. It is these latter changes that have been overlooked by most previous work in the area" (1988, pp. 495–96). Further, the potential of debates will wax or wane as electoral volatility rises or falls. Sears and Chaffee's synthesis of research about debate effects explained, "If increasing numbers of voters wait until the fall campaign to make up their minds, the potential utility of debates . . . will increase in the future" (1979, p. 255).

The body of research on the 1960, 1976, 1980, 1984, and 1988 presidential debates may not be as contradictory as it appears on the surface. For those viewers with clearly defined preferences among candidates, presidential debates tend to strengthen those attitudes, thus exerting a reinforcing effect. For those viewers with weak or no preferences among candidates, debates often help shape or even change their attitudes about candidates, often with sufficient force to alter voting intention. Thus, debates tend to exert considerable influence during the candidate selection process and during general elections featuring a substantial undecided and conflicted vote. The political context in which debates take place determines their potential for influence.

Conclusions

Candidates are conditioned to give answers that meet the requirements of
the medium of television and that will provide good coverage in the
post-event media barrage. Thus, presidential debates in the mass media
age do not live up to their promise of an open exchange between candidates. They instead offer voters more of the same mass-mediated material
packaged differently.

—Political Scientist Diana Owen
(1991, p. 139)

Contemporary presidential debates are *televised events*, a fact which
shapes their form, content, and impact in campaigns. All parties (candidates, academics, interested citizens) must adjust to the debates as
televised communication. Debates still serve the democratic process, but
certainly not in the tradition of the Lincoln-Douglas model. On the basis
of our analysis of the history of past presidential debates, their formats,
the verbal and visual content, and their perceived effects, we offer the
following conclusions.

1. Presidential campaigns have witnessed a dramatic proliferation of
primary debates, with twice as many in the 1984 campaign as in the 1980
campaign, and nearly three times as many in the 1988 campaign as in
the 1984 campaign.

2. Intraparty primary debates have varied widely in their formats and
have been almost without exception more informal and less rigid than
their bipartisan counterparts.

3. Intraparty primary debates are often *television debates*, while interparty general election debates have always been *televised debates*.

4. Opening statements have been utilized infrequently in presidential debates, notable exceptions being the first and fourth 1960 Kennedy-Nixon debates and the 1976 Mondale-Dole vice-presidential debate.

5. Closing statements have been a regular feature of intraparty and interparty debates.

6. Formal candidate rebuttal opportunities have been incorporated in all sixteen general election debates, surrebuttals only in the second segment of the 1980 Carter-Reagan debate.

7. Formal follow-up questions have been featured in nearly half of the general election debates (not included in the 1960 Kennedy-Nixon debates, 1976 Mondale-Dole debate, 1980 Reagan-Anderson debate, 1988 Bush-Dukakis debates, or 1988 Bentsen-Quayle debate).

8. General election debates have been often dichotomized into domestic and foreign affairs questions, the 1976 primary debates being the only attempt to structure an entire campaign debate series around specific topics.

9. Formal candidate cross-examination segments were not incorporated in mediated intraparty debates until the 1984 primary season; they have been featured in relatively few intraparty debates and never in interparty debates.

10. The majority of bipartisan debate panelists have been print media journalists (59 percent), as opposed to broadcast media journalists (41 percent).

11. Almost without exception (the 1976 Mondale-Dole debate), the moderators for general election debates have been broadcast journalists, as opposed to print media journalists. (The second 1988 Bush-Dukakis debate was moderated by an individual who had been both.)

12. Primary debates are increasingly utilizing nationally recognized broadcast journalists as moderators in an interrogator role in a relatively unstructured format, with no accompanying panelists.

13. In the 1988 primary season a member of the opposite party sometimes served as the panelist in an intraparty encounter.

14. Although interrogation of candidates by immediate audience members, either directly or indirectly through the moderator, has been a feature in some intraparty debates, it has never been a practice of a bipartisan debate.

15. The majority (ten) of bipartisan debates have been scheduled for 90 minutes, five have been slotted for 60 minutes, and one (the 1976 Mondale-Dole debate) for 75 minutes.

16. Mediated primary debates have been scheduled for as much as 180 minutes (the 1984 Democratic Dartmouth College debate and the 1988 Democratic "Education '88 Forum"), with the number of candidates generally being the determining factor as to the length of the debate (eight being the greatest number of candidates in a mediated intraparty debate).

17. Issues play a role in the debates, but primarily as a means of demonstrating competence and leadership qualities. In most presidential elections, the issue is character or leadership, not one of specific public policy. Broad themes are generally preferred to specific policy stands. To the extent that candidates select specific issues, these are often targeted to a particular target audience (see Friedenberg, 1990, pp. 192–193).

18. Representing the majority party, Democrats seek to stress their party identity in debates, while Republicans offer a more broad-based appeal. Republicans often target ticket splitters and Independents to bolster their vote totals. Furthermore, Republicans in recent years have tried to portray their Democratic opponents as out of the mainstream, or too liberal, in an effort to drive a wedge between Democratic voters and their party's nominee.

19. Debates, because they take place before the entire nation, place a premium on ambiguity and avoidance of controversy. Even if a candidate cannot win a debate, he or she must avoid losing it (see Friedenberg, 1990, p. 193)

20. The panelists have been partly responsible for the shallow nature of issue discussion in the debates, given their tendency to ask trivial, unfocused, and argumentative questions.

21. Incumbents are not necessarily at a disadvantage in debates. Reagan survived 1984, and Bush, who was part of the incumbent administration, survived 1988. The key is how the incumbent administration is perceived by the electorate. If the record is generally positive, the incumbent needs only to defend that record as safe, in contrast to the untested opponent. On the other hand, if the incumbent administration has serious problems, as Ford did in 1976 and Carter did in 1980, the debates provide an opportunity for challengers to prove their presidential safety. The incumbent is forced to make the opponent the issue and risks losing presidential stature in making the attack.

22. Because television communication stresses the visual domain, it places a premium on the pictorial content of debates, but undermines verbal content. The verbal content that does come through consists of brief, catchy, quotable discourse, ideally suited to sound bites that dominate television news coverage of debates. Sound bites are poorly

suited to the more intricate and reasoned appeals required if candidates are to intelligently discuss their recommendations for addressing important problems that confront the nation.

23. Television rewards a more casual and expressive style of communication. This means that contemporary television debates place greater emphasis on source as opposed to content factors, positive relational messages, and nonverbal cues. Candidates who are able to adapt to these demands employ a casual, softer, warmer communication style.

24. Television stresses photographic presentation, which elevates the importance of decisions about staging, camera angle and placement, and candidate and crowd reaction shots.

25. Televised presidential debates produce various effects. Research indicates that debates socialize younger viewers, in essence stimulating their awareness of and interest in political affairs.

26. Research on other effects has produced mixed findings. The prevailing political context is the best explanation for the conflicting findings involving agenda setting, learning, and affect. Generally, presidential debates that occur early—particularly during the candidate selection phase—and that occur later in campaigns featuring a large number of undecided and conflicted voters, exert the greatest impacts on the campaign agenda, viewer learning about candidate qualifications and about issues, and viewer attitudes about candidates. In circumstances like these, debates can exert considerable impact.

Appendix

GENERAL ELECTION DEBATE FORMATS

Debate Description	Debate Format

1960 General Election Debates

First Kennedy-Nixon debate
September 26, 1960
Chicago, IL
Sponsor: CBS
60 minutes

Opening statements: 8 minutes
Question to candidate A
Candidate A Answer: 2½ minutes
Candidate B Rebuttal: 1½ minutes
Closing statements: 3 minutes
No follow-up questions

Second Kennedy-Nixon debate
October 7, 1960
Washington, D.C.
Sponsor: NBC
60 minutes

No opening statements
Same internal structure as first
   Kennedy-Nixon debate
No closing statements

Third Kennedy-Nixon debate
October 13, 1960
Los Angeles/New York
Sponsor: ABC
60 minutes

No opening statements
Same internal structure as first and
   second Kennedy-Nixon debates
No closing statements

Fourth Kennedy-Nixon debate
October 21, 1960
New York
Sponsor: ABC
60 minutes

Opening statements: 8 minutes
Same internal structure as other
Kennedy-Nixon debates
Closing statements: 4½ minutes

Debate Description	Debate Format

1976 General Election Debates

First Carter-Ford debate
September 23, 1976
Philadelphia, PA
Sponsor: League of Women Voters
   Education Fund
90 minutes

No opening statements
Question to Candidate A
Candidate A Answer: 3 minutes
Optional follow-up question to
   Candidate A
Candidate A Answer: 2 minutes
Candidate B Rebuttal: 2 minutes
Closing statements: 3 minutes

Second Carter-Ford debate
October 6, 1976
San Francisco, CA
Sponsor: League of Women Voters
   Education Fund
90 minutes

Same structure as first Carter-Ford
   debate

Mondale-Dole debate
October 15, 1976
Houston, TX
Sponsor: League of Women Voters
   Education Fund
75 minutes

Opening statements: 2 minutes
Question to Candidate A
Candidate A Answer: $2\frac{1}{2}$ minutes
Candidate B Answer: $2\frac{1}{2}$ minutes
Candidate A Rebuttal: 1 minute
Closing statements: 3 minutes
No follow-up questions

Third Carter-Ford debate
October 22, 1976
Williamsburg, VA
Sponsor: League of Women Voters
   Education Fund
90 minutes

No opening statements
Question to Candidate A
Candidate A Answer: $2\frac{1}{2}$ minutes
Optional follow-up question to
   Candidate A
Candidate A Answer: 2 minutes
Candidate B Rebuttal: 2 minutes
Closing statements: 4 minutes

1980 General Election Debates

Reagan-Anderson debate
September 21, 1980
Baltimore, MD
Sponsor: League of Women Voters
   Education Fund
60 minutes

No opening statements
Question to Candidate A
Candidate A Answer: $2\frac{1}{2}$ minutes
Restatement of question
Candidate B Answer: $2\frac{1}{2}$ minutes
Candidate A Rebuttal: $1\frac{1}{4}$ minutes
Candidate B Rebuttal: $1\frac{1}{4}$ minutes
Closing statements: 3 minutes
No follow-up questions

Debate Description

Carter-Reagan debate
October 28, 1980
Cleveland, OH
Sponsor: League of Women Voters
  Education Fund
90 minutes

Debate Format

No opening statements
First Segment
Question to Candidate A
Candidate A Answer: 2 minutes
Follow-up question to Candidate A
Candidate A Answer: 1 minute
Restatement of question
Candidate B Answer: 2 minutes
Follow-up question to Candidate B
Candidate B Answer: 1 minute
Candidate A Rebuttal: 1 minute
Candidate B Rebuttal: 1 minute
Second Segment
Question to Candidate A
Candidate A Answer: 2 minutes
Restatement of question
Candidate B Answer: 2 minutes
Candidate A Rebuttal: 1½ minutes
Candidate B Rebuttal: 1½ minutes
Candidate A Surrebuttal: 1 minute
Candidate B Surrebuttal: 1 minute
Closing statements: 3 minutes

1984 General Election Debates

First Reagan-Mondale debate
October 7, 1984
Louisville, KY
Sponsor: League of Women Voters
  Education Fund
100 minutes

No opening statements
Question to Candidate A
Candidate A Answer: 2½ minutes
Follow-up question to Candidate A
Candidate A Answer: 1 minute
Restatement of question
Candidate B Answer: 2½ minutes
Follow-up question to Candidate B
Candidate B Answer: 1 minute
Candidate A Rebuttal: 1 minute
Candidate B Rebuttal: 1 minute
Closing statements: 4 minutes

Bush-Ferraro debate
October 11, 1984
Philadelphia, PA
Sponsor: League of Women Voters
  Education Fund
90 minutes

No opening statements
Panelist A initial question to
  Candidate A
Candidate A Answer: 2½ minutes
Follow-up question to Candidate A
Candidate A Answer: 1 minute
Panelist A initial question to
  Candidate B

Debate Description	Debate Format
	Candidate B Answer: 2½ minutes
	Follow-up question to Candidate B
	Candidate B Answer: 1 minute
	Candidate A Rebuttal: 1 minute
	Candidate B Rebuttal: 1 minute
	Closing statements: 4 minutes
Second Reagan-Mondale debate October 21, 1984 Kansas City, MO Sponsor: League of Women Voters Education Fund 90 minutes	Same structure as first Reagan-Mondale debate

1988 General Election Debates

Debate Description	Debate Format
First Bush-Dukakis debate September 25, 1988 Winston-Salem, NC Sponsor: Commission on Presidential Debates 90 minutes	No opening statements Panelist A initial question to Candidate A Candidate A Answer: 2 minutes Candidate B Rebuttal: 1 minute Panelist A second question to Candidate B Candidate B Answer: 2 minutes Candidate A Rebuttal: 1 minute Closing statements: 2 minutes
Bentsen-Quayle debate October 5, 1988 Omaha, NE Sponsor: Commission on Presidential Debates 90 minutes	Same structure as first Bush-Dukakis debate
Second Bush-Dukakis debate October 13, 1988 Los Angeles, CA Sponsor: Commission on Presidential Debates 90 minutes	Same structure as first Bush-Dukakis debate

References

Abramowitz, A. I. 1978. The impact of a presidential debate on voter rationality. *American Journal of Political Science, 22,* 680–90.

Adams, W. C. 1983. Media power in presidential elections: An exploratory analysis, 1960–1980. In Adams, W. C. (Ed.), *Television coverage of the 1980 presidential campaign* (161–87). Norwood, NJ: Ablex.

Alexander, H. E., and Margolis, J. 1980. The making of the debates. In Bishop, G. F., Meadow, R. G., and Jackson-Beeck M. (Eds.), *The presidential debates: Media, electoral, and policy perspectives* (18–32). New York: Praeger.

Altheide, D. L., and Snow, R. P. 1979. *Media logic.* Beverly Hills, CA: Sage.

Anderson, J. A., and Avery, R. K. 1978. An analysis of changes in voter perception of candidates' positions. *Communication Monographs, 45,* 354–61.

Argyle, M., Alkema, F., and Gilmour, R. 1971. The communication of friendly and hostile attitudes by verbal and nonverbal signals. *European Journal of Social Psychology, 1,* 385–402.

Argyle, M., Salter, V., Nicholson, H., Williams, M., and Burgess, P. 1970. The communication of superior and inferior attitudes by verbal and nonverbal signals. *British Journal of Social and Clinical Psychology, 9,* 221–31.

Armstrong, R. 1988. *The next hurrah: The communications revolution in American politics.* New York: Beech Tree Books.

Asher, H. 1980. *Presidential elections and American politics: Voters, candidates, and campaigns since 1952.* Revised edition. Homewood, IL: The Dorsey Press.

Atkin, C., Hocking, J., and McDermott, S. 1979. Home state voter response and secondary media coverage. In Kraus, S. (Ed.), *The great debates: Carter vs. Ford, 1976* (pp. 429–36). Bloomington: Indiana University Press.

Atkinson, J. M. 1986. The 1983 election and the demise of live oratory. In Crewe, I and Harrop, M. (Eds.), *Political communications: The general election campaign of 1983* (pp. 38–55). Cambridge University Press.

Atkinson, M. 1984. *Our masters' voices: The language and body language of politics.* London: Methuen.

Auer, J. J. 1977. The counterfeit debates. In Kraus, S. (Ed.), *The great debates: Kennedy vs. Nixon, 1960* (pp. 142–50). Bloomington: Indiana University Press.

Auer, J. J. 1981. Great myths about the great debates. *Speaker and Gavel, 18,* 14–21.

Axelrod, R. 1972. Where the voters are from: An analysis of electoral coalitions, 1952–1968. *American Political Science Review, 66,* 11–20.

Banker, S. R. November 1985. *The hall of mirrors: Candidate's campaign media during and after the presidential debates.* Paper presented at the Speech Communication Association Convention, Denver, CO.

Barber, J. D. 1980. *The pulse of politics: Electing presidents in the media age.* New York: W. W. Norton & Company.

Barnett, G. A. 1981. A multidimensional analysis of the 1976 presidential campaign. *Communication Quarterly, 29,* 156–65.

Bechtolt, W. E., Jr., Hilyard, J., and Bybee, C. R. 1977. Agenda control in the 1976 debates: A content analysis. *Journalism Quarterly, 54,* 674–81.

Becker, L. B., and McCombs, M. E. 1978. The role of the press in determining voter reaction to presidential primaries. *Human Communication Research, 4,* 301–7.

Becker, L. B., Sobowale, I. A., Cobbey, R. E., and Eyal, C. H. 1980. Debates' effects on voters' understanding of candidates and issues. In Bishop, G. F., Meadow, R. G., and Jackson-Beeck, M. (Eds.), *The presidential debates: Media, electoral, and policy perspectives* (pp. 126–39). New York: Praeger.

Becker, L. B., Weaver, D. H., Graber, D. A., and McCombs, M. E. 1979. Influence on public agendas. In Kraus, S. (Ed.), *The great debates: Carter vs. Ford, 1976* (pp. 418–28). Bloomington: Indiana University Press.

Becker, S. L., and Kraus, S. 1978. The study of campaign '76: An overview. *Communication Monographs, 45,* 265–67.

Becker, S. L., Pepper, R., Wenner, L. A., and Kim, J. K. 1979. Information flow and the shaping of meanings. In Kraus, S. (Ed.), *The great debates: Carter vs. Ford, 1976* (pp. 384–97). Bloomington: Indiana University Press.

Beniger, J. R. 1987. Personalization of mass media and the growth of pseudo-community. *Communication Research, 14,* 352–70.

Ben-Zeev, S., and White, I. S. 1977. Effects and implications. In Kraus, S. (Ed.), *The great debates: Kennedy vs. Nixon, 1960* (pp. 331–37). Bloomington: Indiana University Press.

Berelson, B. R., Lazarsfeld, P. F., and McPhee, W. N. 1954. *Voting: A study of opinion formation in a presidential campaign.* Chicago: University of Chicago Press.

Berquist, G. 1990. The 1976 Carter-Ford presidential debates. In Friedenberg, R. V. (Ed.), *Rhetorical studies of national political debates* (pp. 29–44). New York: Praeger.

Berquist, G. F., Jr. 1960. The Kennedy-Humphrey debate. *Today's Speech, 8,* 2–3, 31.

Berquist, G. F., and Golden, J. L. 1981. Media rhetoric, criticism and the public perception of the 1980 presidential debates. *Quarterly Journal of Speech, 67,* 125–37.

Berry, J. P., Jr. 1987. *John F. Kennedy and the media: The first television president.* Lanham, MD: University Press of America Inc.

Birdwhistell, R. L. 1955. Background to kinesics. *ETC, 13,* 10–18.

Bishop, G. F., Oldendick, R. W., and Tuchfarber, A. J. 1978. Debate watching and the acquisition of political knowledge. *Journal of Communication, 28*(4), 99–113.

Bishop, G. F., Oldendick, R. W., and Tuchfarber, A. J. 1980. The presidential debates as a device for increasing the "rationality" of electoral behavior. In Bishop, G. F., Meadow, R. G. and Jackson-Beeck, M. (Eds.), *The presidential debates: Media, electoral, and policy perspectives* (pp. 179–96). New York: Praeger.

Bitzer, L., and Rueter, T. 1980. *Carter vs. Ford: The counterfeit debates of 1976.* Madison: The University of Wisconsin Press.

Blankenship, J., and Fine, M. April 1984. *Debating in a midwestern presidential primary: The 1980 Illinois debate.* Paper presented at the Southern Speech Communication Association Convention, Baton Rouge, LA.

Blankenship, J., Fine, M. G., and Davis, L. K. 1983. The 1980 Republican primary debates: The transformation of actor to scene. *Quarterly Journal of Speech, 69*, 25–36.

Blankenship, J., and Kang, J. G. 1991. *The 1984 presidential and vice-presidential debates: The printed press and "construction" by metaphor. Presidential Studies Quarterly, 21*, 307–18.

Blumler, J. G., and McQuail, D. 1969. *Television in politics: Its uses and influence.* Chicago: University of Chicago Press.

Borgman, J. October 24, 1988. [Cartoon]. *Newsweek*, p. 17.

Bowes, J. E., and Strentz, H. 1979. Candidate images: Stereotyping and the 1976 debates. In Ruben, B. D. (Ed.), *Communication yearbook 2* (pp. 391–406). New Brunswick, NJ: Transaction Books.

Boyd, R. W. 1972. Rejoinder to "comment" by Richard A. Brody, Benjamin I. Page, and John H. Kessel. *American Political Science Review, 66*, 468–70.

Brock, B. L. April 1981. *Contemporary political argument: A dramatistic analysis of the 1980 Reagan-Carter presidential debate.* Paper presented at the Central States Speech Association Convention, Chicago, IL.

Brody, R. A., and Page, B. I. 1972. Comment: An assessment of policy voting. *American Political Science Review, 66*, 450–58.

Brokaw, T. 1987. Networks should sponsor debates. In Swerdlow, J. L. (Ed.), *Presidential debates: 1988 and beyond* (pp. 73–76). Washington, DC: Congressional Quarterly.

Brummett, B. 1988. The homology hypothesis: Pornography on the VCR. *Critical Studies in Mass Communication, 5*, 202–16.

Bryan, F. J. April 1989. *A metaphorical analysis of the 1988 presidential debates.* Paper presented at the Southern States Communication Association Convention, Louisville, KY.

Brydon, S. R. 1979. *The Carter-Ford television debates: A study in campaign communication.* Ph.D. diss., University of Southern California, Los Angeles.

Brydon, S. R. November 1985a. *Reagan vs. Reagan: The incumbency factor in the 1984 presidential debates.* Paper presented at the Speech Communication Association Convention, Denver, CO.

Brydon, S. R. 1985b. The two faces of Jimmy Carter: The transformation of a presidential debater, 1976 and 1980. *Central States Speech Journal, 36*, 138–51.

Brydon, S. R. November 1989. *Spinners on patrol: Network coverage in the aftermath of presidential and vice presidential debates*. Paper presented at the Speech Communication Association Convention, San Francisco, CA.

Brydon, S. R. June 1990a. *The American presidential debates of 1988: A narrative perspective*. Paper presented at the International Communication Association Convention, Dublin, Ireland.

Brydon, S. R. November 1990b. *The expectations game: Presumption in the 1988 presidential and vice-presidential debates*. Paper presented at the Speech Communication Association Convention, Chiago, IL.

Bryski, B. G. 1978. An analysis of evidence in the first Ford/Carter debate. *Journal of Applied Communication Research, 6,* 19–30.

Bulsys, J. A. November 1989. *Televised presidential debates: In search of an evaluative paradigm*. Paper presented at the Speech Communication Association Convention, San Francisco, CA.

Burgoon, J. K. 1980. Nonverbal communication research on the 1970s: An overview. In Nimmo, D. (Ed.), *Communication yearbook 4* (pp. 179–97). New Brunswick, NJ: Transaction Books.

Burgoon, J. K., Buller, D. B., Hale, J. L., and deTurck, M. A. 1984. Relational messages associated with nonverbal behaviors. *Human Comunication Research, 10,* 351–78.

Burgoon, J. K., Buller, D. B., and Woodall, W. G. 1989. *Nonverbal communication: The unspoken dialogue*. New York: Harper & Row.

Burgoon, J. K., and Hale, J. L. 1984. The fundamental topoi of relational communication. *Communication Monographs, 51,* 193–214.

Burgoon, J. K., and Hale, J. L. 1987. Validation and measurement of the fundamental themes in relational communication. *Communication Monographs, 54,* 19–41.

Burgoon, J. K., Pfau, M., Parrott, R., Birk, T., Coker, R., and Burgoon, M. 1987. Relational communication, satisfaction, compliance-gaining strategies, and compliance in communication between physicians and patients. *Communication Monographs, 54,* 307–24.

Burnkrant, R. E., and Sawyer, A. G. 1983. Effects of involvement and message content on information-processing intensity. In Harris, R. J. (Ed.), *Information processing research in advertising* (pp. 43–64). Hillsdale, NJ: Lawrence Erlbaum Associates.

Burns, K. L., and Beier, E. G. 1973. Significance of vocal and visual channels in the decoding of emotional meaning. *Journal of Communication, 23,* 118–30.

Campbell, A., Converse, P. E., Miller, W. E., and Stokes, D. E. 1960. *The American voter*. New York: John Wiley & Sons, Inc.

Campbell, A., Gurin, G., and Miller, W. E. 1954. *The voter decides*. Evanston, IL: Row, Peterson & Co.

Campbell, J. A. 1983. Candidate image evaluations: Influence and rationalization in presidential primaries. *American Politics Quarterly, 11,* 293–313.

Cannon, L. 1991. *President Reagan: The role of a lifetime*. New York: Simon & Schuster.

Carlin, D. P. 1989. A defense of the "debate" in presidential debates. *Argumentation and Advocacy, 25,* 208–13.

Carlin, D. P., and Brown, J. November 1989. *The future sponsorship of presidential debates: What can or should be done.* Paper presented at the Speech Communication Association Convention, San Francisco, CA.

Carpenter, E. 1986. The new languages. In Gumpert, G., and Cathcart, R. (Eds.), *Intermedia: Interpersonal communication in a media world* (3rd edition, pp. 353–67). New York: Oxford University Press.

Casey, G., and Fitzgerald, M. R. October 1977. *Candidate images and the 1976 presidential debates.* Paper presented at the Midwest Association for Public Opinion Research, Chicago, IL.

Cater, D. 1987. A presidential debates commission. In Swerdlow, J. L. (Ed.), *Presidential debates: 1988 and beyond* (pp. 86–88). Washington, DC: Congressional Quarterly.

Chaffee, S. H. 1978. Presidential debates—Are they helpful to voters? *Communication Monographs, 45,* 330–46.

Chaffee, S. H., and Choe, S. Y. 1980. Time of decision and media use during the Ford-Carter campaign. *Public Opinion Quarterly, 44,* 53–69.

Chaffee, S. H., and Dennis, J. 1979. Presidential debates: An empirical assessment. In Ranney, A. (Ed.), *The past present and future of presidential debates* (pp. 75–101). Washington, DC: American Enterprise Institute for Public Policy Research.

Chaiken, S. 1980. Heuristic versus systematic information processing and the use of source versus message cues in persuasion. *Journal of Personality and Social Psychology, 39,* 752–66.

Chaiken, S. 1987. The heuristic model of persuasion. In Zanna, M. P., Olson, J. M., and Herman, C. P. (Eds.), *Social influence: The Ontario Symposium* (Vol. 5, pp. 3–39). Hillsdale, NJ: Lawrence Erlbaum Associates.

Chaiken, S., and Eagly, A. H. 1976. Communication modality as a determinant of message pervasiveness and message comprehensibility. *Journal of Personality and Social Psychology, 34,* 605–14.

Chaiken, S., and Eagly, A. H. 1983. Communication modality as a determinant of persuasion: The role of communicator salience. *Journal of Personality and Social Psychology, 45,* 241–56.

Cheney, R. B. 1979. The 1976 presidential debates: A Republican perspective. In Ranney, A. (Ed.), *The past and future of presidential debates* (pp. 107–130). Washington, DC: American Enterprise Institute for Public Policy Research.

Chesebro, J. W. 1984. The media reality: Epistemological functions of media in cultural systems. *Critical Studies in Mass Communication, 1,* 111–30.

Cheshire, D. May 1989. *The expectation game and presidential debate: Is argument quality declining?* Paper presented at the Eastern Communication Association Convention, Ocean City, MD.

Church, G. J. October 22, 1984a. Getting a second look: The debate gives Mondale a boost—but not a bonanza. *Time,* pp. 23–28.

Church, G. J. October 29, 1984b. Debating the debates: Does the present format produce insights or distortions? *Time,* pp. 31–32.

Clark, E. 1988. *The want makers: The world of advertising: How they make you buy.* New York: Viking Penguin Inc.

Clendinen, D. November 11, 1984. Mondale—A man out of step in an era of television politics. *Arizona Daily Star,* p. 4A.

Cleveland, L. 1969. Symbols and politics: Mass communication and the public drama. *Politics: Australian Political Studies Association Journal, 4,* 186–96.

Cohen, A. A. 1976. Radio vs. TV: The effect of the medium. *Journal of Communication, 26(2),* 29–35.

Cundy, D. T., and Havick, J. J. March 1977. *Impact of the 1976 presidential debates: A preliminary analysis.* Paper presented at the Western Political Science Association Convention, Los Angeles, CA.

Dates set for debates. September 9, 1988. *Kansas City Times,* p. A3.

Davis, D. K. (1979). Influence on vote decisions. In Kraus, S. (Ed.), *The great debates: Carter vs. Ford, 1976* (pp. 331–47). Bloomington: Indiana University Press.

Davis, L. K. 1978. Camera-eye contact by the candidates in the presidential debates of 1976. *Journalism Quarterly, 55,* 431–37, 455.

Davis, M. H. 1982. Voting intentions and the 1980 Carter-Reagan debate. *Journal of Applied Social Psychology, 12,* 481–92.

Deatherage, S. November 1990. *The uncertain role of debates in presidential primaries.* Paper presented at the Speech Communication Association Convention, Chicago, IL.

deBock, H. 1978. Influence of the Ford-Carter debates on Dutch TV viewers. *Journalism Quarterly, 55,* 583–85.

Decker, W. D. November 1981. *The League of Women Voters: Sponsorship promotion and definition of public political debate.* Paper presented at the Speech Communication Association Convention, Anaheim, CA.

Decker, W. D. 1990. The 1988 Quayle-Bentson vice-presidential debate. In Friedenberg, R. V. (Ed.), *Rhetorical studies of national political debates* (pp. 167–86). New York: Praeger.

Dennis, J., Chaffee, S. H., and Choe, S. Y. 1979. Impact on partisan, image, and issue voting. In Kraus, S. (Ed.), *The great debates: Carter vs. Ford, 1976* (pp. 314–30). Bloomington: Indiana University Press.

Desmond, R. J., and Donohue, T. R. 1981. The role of the 1976 televised presidential debates in the political socialization of adolescents. *Communication Quarterly, 29,* 302–08.

DeStephen, D. 1981. *Value images in presidential debates: A comparative study of 1976 and 1980.* Manuscript.

DeVries, W., and Tarrance, V. L. 1972. *The ticket-splitter: A new force in American politics.* Grand Rapids, MI: William B. Eerdmans Publishing Co.

Diamond, E., and Friery, K. 1987. Media coverage of presidential debates. In Swerdlow, J. L. (Ed.), *Presidential debates: 1988 and beyond* (pp. 43–51). Washington, DC: Congressional Quarterly.

Dillin, J. October 25, 1984. Audience in the hall saw a "different debate" last Sunday. *The Christian Science Monitor,* pp. 3–4.

Donatelli, F. J., and Francis, L. C. 1987. Sponsorship of presidential debates: Who does it? Who cares? In Swerdlow, J. L. (Ed.), *Presidential debates: 1988 and beyond* (pp. 58–65). Washington, DC: Congressional Quarterly.

Drew, D., and Weaver, D. June 1990. *Voter learning in the 1988 presidential election: Did the debates and the media matter?* Paper presented at the International Communication Association Convention, Dublin, Ireland.

Drew, E. 1981. *Portrait of an election: The 1980 presidential campaign.* New York: Simon & Schuster.

Drew, E. 1985. *Campaign journal: The political events of 1983–1984. New York: Macmillan.*

Drucker, S. J. November 1989. *Televised presidential debates: A new tradition.* Paper presented at the Speech Communication Association Convention, San Francisco, CA.

Drucker, S. J., and Hunold, J. P. 1987. The debating game. *Critical Studies in Mass Communication, 4,* 202–7.

Eadie, W. F., Krivonos, P. D., and Goodman, G. April 1977. *Winners and losers: Credibility and the first debate.* Paper presented at the Central States Speech Association Convention, Southfield, MI.

Ellsworth, J. W. 1965. Rationality and campaigning: A content analysis of the 1960 presidential campaign debates. *The Western Political Quarterly, 43,* 794–802.

Erlich, H. S. May 1985. *A linguistic analysis of Ronald Reagan in the first 1984 debate.* Paper presented at the Eastern Communication Association Convention, Providence, RI.

Farah, B. G., and Klein, E. 1989. Public opinion trends. In Pomper, G. M. (Ed.), *The election of 1988: Reports and interpretations* (pp. 103–28). Chatham, NJ: Chatham House Publishers, Inc.

Feigert, F. B., and Bowling, W. J. April 1980. *The impact of televised debates on the 1976 presidential election: New myths and old realities.* Paper presented at the annual meeting of the Midwest Political Science Association, Chicago, IL.

Ferguson, E. B. October 8, 1984. Mondale kept Reagan off balance, but president didn't slip. *Arizona Daily Star,* pp. 1–2.

Ferguson, M. A., Hollander, B. A., and Melwani, G. May 1989. *The "dampening effect" of post debate commentary: The Bentsen-Quayle debate.* Paper presented at the International Communication Association Convention, San Francisco, CA.

Fish, M. May 1989. *Deconstructing the 1988 presidential debates.* Paper presented at the International Communication Association Convention, San Francisco, CA.

5 candidates call foreign aid vital. May 2, 1952. *New York Times,* p. 13.

Frana, A. W. 1989. Characteristics of effective argumentation. *Argumentation and Advocacy, 25,* 200–202.

Freeman, W. 1981. The way of righteousness vs. the voice of the turtle: The Carter-Reagan debate? *Exetasis, 6,* 14–24.

Friedenberg, R. V. 1990. Patterns and trends in national political debates 1960–1988. In Friedenberg, R. V. (Ed.), *Rhetorical studies of national political debates* (pp. 187–210). New York: Praeger.

Frye, J. K., and Bryski, B. G. March 1978. *Accident and design: Implications of technical and functional factors of network television coverage of the Ford/ Carter presidential debates.* Paper presented at the Eastern Communication Association Convention, Boston, MA.

Frye, J. K., Goldhaber, G. M., and Bryski, B. G. May 1981. *A communication analysis of selected nonverbal dimensions of the 1980 Carter/Reagan presidential debate.* Paper presented at the International Communication Association Convention, Minneapolis, MN.

Fulk, J., Steinfeld, C. W., Schmitz, J., and Power, J. G. 1987. A social information processing model of media use in organizations. *Communication Research, 14*, 529–52.

Geer, J. G. April 1987. *The effects of presidential debates on the electorate's preferences for candidates.* Paper presented at the Midwest Political Science Association Convention, Chicago, IL.

Geer, J. G. 1988. The effects of presidential debates on the electorate's preferences for candidates. *American Politics Quarterly, 16*, 486–501.

Germond, J. W., and Witcover, J. 1979. Presidential debates: An overview. In Ranney, A. (Ed.), *The past and future of presidential debates* (pp. 191–205). Washington, DC: American Enterprise Institute for Public Policy Research.

Germond, J. W., and Witcover, J. 1989. *Whose broad stripes and bright stars: The trivial pursuit of the presidency 1988.* New York: Warner Books.

Gerstle, J. 1979. The study of campaign debating on television: A comparative analysis of U.S. and French approaches—A French perspective. *Political Communication Review, 4*, 34–40.

Gitter, A. G., Black, H., and Fishman, J. E. 1975. Effect of race, sex, nonverbal communication, and verbal communication on perception of leadership. *Sociology and Social Research, 60*, 46–57.

Gold, E. R. 1988. Ronald Reagan and the oral tradition. *Central States Speech Journal, 39*, 159–76.

Goldhaber, G. M., Frye, J. K., Porter, D. T., and Yates, M. P. April 1977. *The image of the candidates: A communication analysis of the Ford/Carter debates, I, II, III.* Paper presented at the Kinesics Conference, Fairleigh Dickinson University, Madison, NJ.

Goldman, P., and Fuller, T. 1985. *The quest for the presidency 1984.* New York: Bantam Books.

Gopoian, J. D. 1982. Issue preference and candidate choice in presidential primaries. *American Journal of Political Science, 26*, 524–46.

Govang, D., and Ritter, K. October 1981. *Reagan vs. Carter: A progress report on a content analysis of the "main points" in the 1980 presidential debates.* Paper presented at the Rhetoric Conference of the Southern Speech Communication Association and the Central States Speech Association, Austin Peay State University, Clarksville, TN.

Graber, D. A. 1976. Press and TV as opinion resources in presidential campaigns. *Public Opinion Quarterly, 40*, 285–303.

Graber, D. A. 1980a. *Mass media and American politics.* Washington, DC: Congressional Quarterly.

Graber, D. A. 1980b. Problems in measuring audience effects of the 1976 debates. In Bishop, G. F., Meadow, R. G., and Jackson-Beeck, M. (Eds.), *The presidential debates: Media, electoral, and policy perspectives* (pp. 105–25). New York: Praeger.

Graber, D. A. 1981. Political languages. In Nimmo, D., and Sanders, K. R. (Eds.), *Handbook of political communication* (pp. 195–223). Beverly Hills, CA: Sage.

Graber, D. A. 1987. Television news without pictures? *Critical Studies in Mass Communication, 4*, 74–78.

Graber, D. A., and Kim, Y. Y. 1978. Why John Q. Voter did not learn much from the 1976 presidential debates. In Rubin, B. D. (Ed.), *Communication yearbook 2* (pp. 407–21). New Brunswick, NJ: Transaction Books.

Gravlee, G. J., Irvine, J. R., and Vancil, D. L. 1976. The final Ford-Carter Debate: A rhetoric of rescue. *Exetasis, 3*, 24–32.

Greenfield, J. 1982. *The real campaign: How the media missed the story of the 1980 campaign.* New York: Summit Books.

Gregg, R. B. 1977. The rhetoric of political newscasting. *Central States Speech Journal, 28*, 221–37.

Gronbeck, B. E. November 1989. *Negative narratives in 1988 presidential campaign ads.* Paper presented at the Speech Communication Association Convention, San Francisco, CA.

Gunter, B. 1980. Remembering television news: Effects of picture content. *The Journal of General Psychology, 102*, 127–33.

Hagner, P. R., and Rieselbach, L. N. 1980. The impact of the 1976 presidential debates: Conversion or reinforcement? In Bishop, G. F., Meadow, R. G., and Jackson-Beeck, M. (Eds.), *The presidential debates: Media, electoral, and policy perspectives* (pp. 157–78). New York: Praeger.

Hahn, D. 1970. The effect of TV on presidential campaigns. *Today's Speech, 19*, 4–17.

Hahn, D. F., and Goncher, R. M. 1972. Political myth: The image and the issue. *Today's Speech, 20*, 57–65.

Hardy-Short, D. November 1985. *An insider's view of the constraints affecting Geraldine Ferraro's preparation for the 1984 vice-presidential debate.* Paper presented at the Speech Communication Association Convention, Denver, CO.

Harian, V. October 21, 1988. Telephone interview conducted by senior author. Washington, DC.

Harral, H. B. April 1984. *Debating in a northern presidential primary: New Hampshire in 1980 and 1984.* Paper presented at the Southern Speech Communication Association Convention, Baton Rouge, LA.

Harris, L. October 31, 1980. Reagan won debate, poll shows. *St. Paul Pioneer Press*, pp. 1, 6.

Hawkins, R. P., Pingree, S., Smith, K. A., and Bechtolt, W. E., Jr. 1979. Adolescents' responses to issues and images. In Kraus, S. (Ed.), *The great debates: Carter vs. Ford, 1976* (pp. 368–83). Bloomington: Indiana University Press.

Haynes, W. L. 1988. Of that which we cannot write: Some notes on the phenomenology of media. *Quarterly Journal of Speech, 74*, 71–101.

Hellweg, S. A. November 1984. *The relationship of imposed format structures and emergent candidate verbal behaviors: A comparison of the 1984 primary and general election debates.* Paper presented at the Speech Communication Association Convention, Chicago, IL.

Hellweg, S. A., and Kugler, D. B. November 1985. *A rhetorical analysis of the 1984 Bush-Ferraro vice presidential debate.* Paper presented at the Speech Communication Association Convention, Denver, CO.

Hellweg, S. A., and Phillips, S. L. 1981a. Form and substance: A comparative analysis of five formats used in the 1980 presidential debates. *Speaker and Gavel, 18*, 67–76.

Hellweg, S. A., and Phillips, S. L. 1981b. A verbal and visual analysis of the 1980 Houston Republican presidential primary debate. *Southern Speech Communication Journal, 47,* 23–28.

Hellweg, S. A., and Stevens, M. D. November 1990. *Argumentative strategies in the vice-presidential debates: 1976, 1984, and 1988.* Paper presented at the Speech Communication Association Convention, Chicago, IL.

Hellweg, S. A., and Verhoye, A. M. November 1989. *A comparative verbal analysis of the two 1988 Bush-Dukakis presidential debates.* Paper presented at the Speech Communication Association Convention, San Francisco, CA.

Henry, W. A., III. October 22, 1984. In search of questioners: The league runs into problems putting together a panel. *Time,* p. 84.

Henry, W. A. III. 1985. *Visions of America: How we saw the 1984 election.* Boston: Atlantic Monthly Press.

Herbeck, D. May 1989. *The benevolent technocrat: Michael Dukakis' strategy in the 1988 presidential debates.* Paper presented at the Eastern Communication Association Convention, Ocean City, MD.

Hershey, M. R. 1989. The campaign and the media. In Pomper, G. M. (Ed.), *The election of 1988: Reports and interpretations* (pp. 73–102). Chatham, NJ: Chatham House Publishers, Inc.

Highlander, J. P., and Watkins, L. I. 1962. A closer look at the great debates. *Western Speech, 26,* 39–48.

Hinck, E. A. November 1988. *Enacting the presidency: Political debates as dramatic enactment of presidential character.* Paper presented at the Speech Communication Association Convention, New Orleans, LA.

Hinck, E. A. November 1989. *Dramatic enactment of presidential character in the presidential debates of 1988.* Paper presented at the Speech Communication Association Convention, San Francisco, CA.

Hinck, E. A. November 1990. *The role of the 1984 vice-presidential debate in the presidential campaign.* Paper presented at the Speech Communication Association Convention, Chicago, IL.

Hofstetter, C. R., Zukin, C., and Buss, T. F. 1978. Political imagery and information in an age of television. *Journalism Quarterly, 55,* 562–69.

Hogan, J. M. 1989. Media nihilism and the presidential debates. *Argumentation and Advocacy, 25,* 220–25.

Horton, D., and Wohl, R. R. 1956. Mass communication and parasocial interaction: Observations on intimacy at a distance. *Psychiatry, 19,* 215–29.

Hyman, H. 1959. *Political socialization.* Glencoe, IL: The Free Press.

In the heat of the kitchen. October 8, 1984. *Time,* pp. 18–24.

Ivie, R. L., and Ritter, K. November 1988. *Whither the evil empire? Reagan and the presidential candidates debating foreign policy in the 1988 campaign.* Paper presented at the Speech Communication Association Convention, New Orleans, LA.

Jackson-Beeck, M., and Meadow, R. G. 1979a. The triple agenda of presidential debates. *Public Opinion Quarterly, 43,* 173–80.

Jackson-Beeck, M., and Meadow, R. G. 1979b. Content analysis of televised communication events: The presidential debates. *Communication Research, 6,* 321–44.

Jamieson, K. H. 1984. *Packaging the presidency: A history and criticism of presidential campaign advertising.* New York: Oxford University Press.

Jamieson, K. H. 1988. *Eloquence in an electronic age: The transformation of political speech making.* New York: Oxford University Press.

Jamieson, K. H. 1989. Context and the creation of meaning in the advertising of the 1988 presidential campaign. *American Behavioral Scientist, 32,* 415–24.

Jamieson, K. H., and Birdsell, D. S. 1988. *Presidential debates: The challenge of creating an informed electorate.* New York: Oxford University Press.

Kaid, L. L., and Davidson, D. K. 1986. Elements of videostyle: Candidate presentation through television advertising. In Kaid, L. L., Nimmo, D., and Sanders, K. R. (Eds.), *New perspectives on political advertising* (pp. 184–209). Carbondale: Southern Illinois University Press.

Kaid, L. L., and Sanders, K. R. 1985. Survey of political communication theory and research. In Sanders, K. R., Kaid, L. L., and Nimmo, D. (Eds.), *Political communication yearbook: 1984* (pp. 283–308). Carbondale: Southern Illinois University Press.

Kalb, M. December 1989. *A proposal on presidential debates.* Paper presented at the Conference on Presidential Debates, Washington, DC.

Katz, E., and Feldman, J. J. 1977. The debates in light of research: A survey of surveys. In Kraus, S. (Ed.), *The great debates: Kennedy vs. Nixon, 1960* (pp. 173–223). Bloomington: Indiana University Press.

Katz, E., and Lazarsfeld, P. F. 1955. *Personal influence: The part played by people in the flow of mass communication.* New York: Free Press.

Kay, J. November 1983. *Political campaign debates: Reconciling public, media, and candidate needs.* Paper presented at the Speech Communication Association Convention, Washington, DC.

Kay, J. November 1984. *A narrative study of the 1984 presidential debates.* Paper presented at the Speech Communication Association Convention, Chicago, IL.

Keating, J. P., and Latane, B. 1976. Politicians on TV: The image is the message. *Journal of Social Issues, 32,* 116–31.

Keeter, S. 1987. The illusion of intimacy: Television and the role of candidate personal qualities in voter choice. *Public Opinion Quarterly, 51,* 344–58.

Kell, C. L. 1976. Round II: The rhetoric of the oval office vs. the rhetoric of the "fireside chat." *Exetasis, 3,* 10–15.

Kelley, S., Jr. 1960. *Political campaigning: Problems in creating an informed electorate.* Washington, DC: Brookings Institution.

Kelley, S., Jr. 1962. Campaign debates: Some facts and issues. *Public Opinion Quarterly, 26,* 351–66.

Kelley, S., Jr. 1983. *Interpreting elections.* Princeton, NJ: Princeton University Press.

Kelley, S., Jr., and Mirer, T. W. 1974. The simple act of voting. *American Political Science Review, 68,* 572–91.

Kemp, R. November 1987. *Let the "Times" report but let the people determine winner of candidates on joint appearances.* Paper presented at the Speech Communication Association Convention, Boston, MA.

Kennamer, J. D., and Chaffee, S. H. 1982. Communication of political information during early presidential primaries: Cognition, affect, and uncertainty. In Burgoon, M. (Ed.), *Communication yearbook 5* (pp. 627–50). New Brunswick, NJ: Transaction Books.

Kepplinger, H. M., and Donsbach, W. 1987. The influence of camera perspectives on the perception of a politician by supporters, opponents, and neutral viewers. In Paletz, D. L. (Ed.), *Political communication research: Approaches, studies, assessments* (pp. 62–72). Norwood, NJ: Ablex.

Kern, M. 1989. *30-second politics: Political advertising in the eighties.* New York: Praeger.

Kilpatrick, C. May 5, 1960. 2 see eye to eye except on taxes. *Washington Post,* p. 1.

Kinder, D. R. 1978. Political person perception: An asymmetrical influence of sentiment and choice on perceptions of presidential candidates. *Journal of Personality and Social Psychology, 8,* 859–71.

Kingdon, J. W. 1966. *Candidates for office: Beliefs and strategies.* New York: Random House.

Kirkpatrick, E. M. 1979. Presidential candidate "debates": What can we learn from 1969? In Ranney, A. (Ed.), *The past and future of presidential debates* (pp. 1–50). Washington, DC: American Enterprise Institute for Public Policy Research.

Kirkpatrick, S. A., Lyons, W., and Fitzgerald, M. R. 1975. Candidates, parties, and issues in the American electorate: Two decades of change. *American Politics Quarterly, 3,* 231–40.

Kraus, S. 1964. Presidential debates in 1964. *Quarterly Journal of Speech, 50,* 19–23.

Kraus, S. 1977. *The great debates: Kennedy vs. Nixon, 1960.* Bloomington: Indiana University Press.

Kraus, S. 1987. Voters win. *Critical Studies in Mass Communication, 4,* 214–16.

Kraus, S. 1988. *Televised presidential debates and public policy.* Hillsdale, NJ: Lawrence Erlbaum Associates.

Kraus, S., and Davis, D. 1976. *The effects of mass communication on political behavior.* University Park: Penn State University Press.

Kraus, S., and Davis, D. K. November 1981. *Televised political debates: The negotiated format.* Paper presented at the Speech Communication Association Convention, Anaheim, CA.

Krauss, R. M., Apple, W., Morency, N., Wenzel, C., and Winton, W. 1981. Verbal, vocal and visible factors in judgments of another's affect. *Journal of Personality and Social Psychology, 40,* 312–19.

Krivonos, P. D. 1976. The first debate: Ford versus Carter—A behavioral criticism. *Exetasis, 3,* 3–9.

Krugman, H. E. 1965. The impact of television advertising: Learning without involvement. *Public Opinion Quarterly, 29,* 349–56.

Krugman, H. E. 1971. Brain wave measures of media involvement. *Journal of Advertising Research, 11,* 3–9.

Kymlicka, B. B., and Matthews, J. 1988. *The Reagan revolution?* Chicago: Dorsey Press

Ladd, E. C., and Ferree, G. D. December/January 1981. Were the pollsters really wrong? *Public Opinion,* pp. 13–20.

Lampl, P. 1979. The sponsor: The League of Women Voters Education Fund. In Kraus, S. (Ed.), *The great debates: Carter vs. Ford, 1976* (pp. 83–104). Bloomington: Indiana University Press.

Lang, G. E. 1987. Still seeking answers. *Critical Studies in Mass Communication, 4,* 211–14.

Lang, G. E., and Lang, K. 1980. The formation of public opinion: Direct and mediated effects of the first debate. In Bishop, G. F., Meadow, R. G., and Jackson-Beeck, M. (Eds.), *The presidential debates: Media, electoral, and policy perspectives* (pp. 61–80). New York: Praeger.

Lang, G. E., and Lang, K. 1984. *Politics and television re-viewed.* Beverly Hills, CA: Sage.

Lang, K., and Lang, G. E. 1968. *Politics and television.* Chicago: Quadrangle Books.

Lang, K., and Lang, G. E. 1977. Reactions of viewers. In Kraus, S. (Ed.), *The great debates: Carter vs. Ford, 1976* (pp. 313–30). Bloomington: Indiana University Press.

Larson, C. U. 1982. Media metaphors: Two perspectives for the rhetorical criticism of TV commercials. *Central States Speech Journal, 33,* 533–46.

Lazarsfeld, P. F., Berelson, B., and Gaudet, H. 1968. *The people's choice: How the voter makes up his mind in a presidential campaign* (3rd ed.). New York: Columbia University Press.

League of Women Voters. October 3, 1988. [Statement by Nancy M. Neuman, president, League of Women Voters]. Press release.

League of Women Voters November 1989. *The League of Women Voters' perspective on presidential debate sponsorship.* Paper presented at the Speech Communication Association Convention, San Francisco, CA.

Lemert, J. B., Elliott, W. R., Nestvold, K. J., and Rarick, G. R. 1983. Effects of viewing a presidential primary debate: An experiment. *Communication Research, 10,* 155–73.

Lemert, J. B., Rosenberg, W. L., Elliott, W. R., Bernstein, J. M., and Nestvold, K. J. May 1989. *Impact of the Bentsen/Quayle debate and of news "verdicts" about the debate: A time-series analysis.* Paper presented at the American Association of Public Opinion Research Convention, St. Petersburg, FL.

Leo, J. November 12, 1984. Not by issues alone: Psychologists explore what makes voters decide. *Time,* p. 37.

Leon, M., and Allen, T. H. June 1990. *Declaring a winner: A contextual analysis of the 1988 presidential debates.* Paper presented at the International Communication Association Convention, Dublin, Ireland.

Lesher, S., Caddell, P., and Rafshoon, G. 1979. Did the debates help Jimmy Carter? In Ranney, A. (Ed.), *The past and future of presidential debates* (pp. 137–46). Washington, DC: American Enterprise Institute for Public Policy Research.

Leuthold, D. A., and Valentine, D. C. 1981. How Reagan "won" the Cleveland debate: Audience predispositions and presidential debate "winners." *Speaker and Gavel, 18,* 60–66.

Levy, M. R. 1979. Watching TV news as para-social interaction. *Journal of Broadcasting, 23,* 69–80.

Linsky, M. 1983. *Television and the presidential elections: Self interest and the public interest.* Lexington, MA: Lexington Books.

Lippmann, W. 1922. *Public opinion.* New York: Macmillan.

Lubell, S. 1977. Personalities vs. issues. In Kraus, S. (Ed.), *The great debates: Kennedy vs. Nixon, 1960* (pp. 151–62). Bloomington: Indiana University Press.

Lupfer, M. B., and Wald, K. D. 1979. An experimental study of the first Carter-Ford debate. *Experimental Study of Politics, 7,* 20–40.

Magnuson, E., and Church, G. J. October 29, 1984. A tie goes to the Gipper. *Time*, pp. 22–26.

Martel, M. 1981. Debate preparations in the Reagan camp: An insider's view. *Speaker and Gavel, 19*, 34–46.

Martel, M. 1983. *Political campaign debates: Images, strategies, and tactics*. New York: Longman.

Mazo, E., Moos, M., Hoffman, H., and Wheeler, H. 1962. *The great debates: An occasional paper on the role of the political process in a free society*. Santa Barbara, CA: Center for the Study of Democratic Institutions.

McBath, J. H., and Fisher, W. R. 1969. Persuasion in presidential campaign communication. *Quarterly Journal of Speech, 55*, 17–25.

McCall, J. M. 1984. The panelists as pseudo-debaters: An evaluation of the questions and questioners in the presidential debates of 1980. *Journal of the American Forensic Association, 21*, 97–104.

McClain, T. B. 1989. Secondary school debate pedagogy. *Argumentation and Advocacy, 25*, 203–04.

McGinniss, J. 1969. *The selling of the president 1968*. New York: Trident Press.

McLeod, J. M., Durall, J. A., Ziemke, D. A., and Bybee, C. A. 1979. Reactions of young and older voters: Expanding the context of effects. In Kraus, S. (Ed.), *The great debates: Carter vs. Ford, 1976* (pp. 348–67). Bloomington: Indiana University Press.

McLuhan, M. 1964. *Understanding media: The extensions of man*. New York: McGraw-Hill.

McMahan, E. M. 1976. Nonverbal communication as a function of attribution in impression formation. *Communication Monographs, 43*, 287–94.

McQuail, D., Blumler, J. G., and Brown, J. R. 1972. The television audience: A revised perspective. In D. McQuail (Ed.), *Sociology of mass communication* (pp. 135–65). Harmondsworth, England: Penguin.

Meadow, R. G. 1983. Televised presidential debates as whistle stop speeches. In Adams, W. C. (Ed.), *Televised coverage of the 1980 presidential campaign* (pp. 89–102). Norwood, NJ: Ablex.

Meadow, R. G. 1987. A speech by any other name. *Critical Studies in Mass Communication, 4*, 207–10.

Meadow, R. G. November 1989. *The triple agenda of presidential debates revised: Audience and the implications of sponsorship*. Paper presented at the Speech Communication Association Convention, San Francisco, CA.

Meadow, R. G., and Jackson-Beeck, M. 1978. Issue evolution: A new perspective on presidential debates. *Journal of Communication, 28*(4), 84–92.

Meadow, R. G., and Jackson-Beeck, M. 1980. A comparative perspective on presidential debates: Issue evolution in 1960 and 1976. In Bishop, G. F., Meadow, R. G., and Jackson-Beeck, M. (Eds.), *The presidential debates: Media, electoral, and policy perspectives* (pp. 33–58). New York: Praeger.

Mehrabian, A. 1971. *Silent messages*. Belmont, CA: Wadsworth.

Mendelsohn, H., and O'Keefe, G. J. 1976. *The people choose a president*. New York: Praeger.

Messaris, P., Eckman, B., and Gumpert, G. 1979. Editing structure in the televised versions of the 1976 presidential debates. *Journal of Broadcasting, 23*, 359–69.

Meyrowitz, J. 1985. *No sense of place: The impact of electronic media on social behavior.* New York: Oxford University Press.

Meyrowitz, J. 1986. Television and interpersonal behavior: Codes of perception and response. In Gumpert, G. and Cathcart, R. (Eds.), *Intermedia: Interpersonal communication in a media world* (3rd edition, pp. 253-72). New York: Oxford University Press.

Mickelson, S. 1972. Face to face: The televised debate. In Mickelson, S. (Ed.), *The electric mirror* (pp. 193-216). New York: Dodd, Mead.

Mickelson, S. 1989. *From whistle stop to sound bite: Four decades of politics and television.* New York: Praeger.

Middleton, R. 1962. National television debates and presidential voting decisions. *Public Opinion Quarterly, 26,* 426-28.

Miller, A. H., and MacKuen, M. 1979. Informing the electorate: A national study. In Kraus, S. (Ed.), *The great debates: Carter vs. Ford, 1976* (pp. 269-97). Bloomington: Indiana University Press.

Miller, W. E., and Levitan, T. E. 1976. *Leadership and change: The new politics and the American electorate.* Cambridge: Winthrop Publishers, Inc.

Minow, N. N., and Sloan, C. M. 1987. Political parties should sponsor political debates. In Swerdlow, J. L. (Ed.), *Presidential debates: 1988 and beyond* (pp. 69-72). Washington, DC: Congressional Quarterly.

Morello, J. T. December 1980. *An analysis of the news media's analysis of the Carter-Reagan debate.* Paper presented to the Metropolitan Washington, DC Communication Association, Washington, DC.

Morello, J. T. 1988a. Argument and visual structuring in the 1984 Reagan-Mondale debates: The medium's influence on the perception of clash. *Western Journal of Speech Communication, 52,* 277-90.

Morello, J. T. 1988b. Visual structuring of the 1976 and 1984 nationally televised presidential debates: Implications. *Central States Speech Journal, 39,* 233-43.

Morello, J. T. November 1990. *Argument and visual structuring in the 1988 Bush-Dukakis presidential campaign debates.* Paper presented at the Speech Communication Association Convention, Chicago, IL.

Morrow, G. R. 1977. Changes in perceptions of Ford and Carter following the first presidential debate. *Perceptual and Motor Skills, 45,* 423-29.

Mortensen, C. D. 1968. The influence of television on policy discussion. *Quarterly Journal of Speech, 54,* 277-81.

Mulder, R. D. 1978. The political effects of the Carter-Ford debate: An experimental analysis. *Sociological Focus, 11,* 33-45.

Murphy, J. M. November 1990. *Presidential debates and campaign rhetoric: Text within context.* Paper presented at the Speech Communication Association Convention, Chicago, IL.

Napolitan, J. 1972. *The election game and how to win it.* New York: Doubleday & Company, Inc.

Nesbit, D. D. 1988. *Videostyle in senate campaigns.* Knoxville: The University of Tennessee Press.

Nessen, R. 1978. *It sure looks different from the inside.* Chicago: Playboy Press.

Neuman, N. M., and Harian, V. 1987. The League of Women Voters should sponsor debates. In Swerdlow, J. L. (Ed.), *Presidential debates: 1988 and beyond* (pp. 77-81). Washington, DC: Congressional Quarterly.

Newcomb, H. 1982. *Television: The critical view* (3rd edition). New York: Oxford University Press.

Newton, D. A., Burgoon, J. K., and Traynowicz, L. L. November 1989. *Relational message interpretations of conversational involvement: Comparing encoding and decoding perspectives.* Paper presented at the Speech Communication Association Convention, San Francisco, CA.

Nie, N. H., and Anderson, K. 1976. Mass belief systems revisited: Political change and attitude structure. In Dryer, E. C. and Rosenbaum, W. A. (Eds.), *Political opinion and behavior: Essays and studies* (3rd edition, pp. 289–324). North Scituate, MA: Duxbury Press.

Nie, N. H., Verba, S., and Petrocik, J. R. 1976. *The changing American voter.* Cambridge: Harvard University Press.

Nimmo, D. 1970. *The political persuaders: The techniques of modern election campaigns.* Englewood Cliffs, NJ: Prentice-Hall.

Nimmo, D., and Combs, J. E. 1983. *Mediated political realities.* New York: Longman.

Nimmo, D., and Mansfield, M. W. November 1985. *Change and persistence in candidate images: Presidential debates across 1976, 1980, and 1984.* Paper presented at the Speech Communication Association Convention, Denver, CO.

Now, a few words in closing. November 10, 1980. *Time,* p. 18.

Oft-Rose, N. 1989. The importance of ethos. *Argumentation and Advocacy, 25,* 197–99.

O'Keefe, G. J. 1975. Political campaigns and mass communication research. In Chaffee, S. H. (Ed.), *Political communication: Issues and strategies for research* (pp. 129–64). Beverly Hills: Sage.

O'Keefe, G. J., and Atwood, L. E. 1981. Communication and election campaigns. In Nimmo, D. D. and Sanders, K. R. (Eds.), *Handbook of political communication* (pp. 329–57). Beverly Hills, CA: Sage.

O'Keefe, G. J., and Mendelsohn, H. 1979. Media influences and their anticipation. In Kraus, S. (Ed.), *The great debates: Carter vs. Ford, 1976* (pp. 405–17). Bloomington: Indiana University Press.

Ornstein, N. 1987. Nonpresidential debates in America. In Swerdlow, J. L. (Ed.), *Presidential debates: 1988 and beyond* (pp. 52–61). Washington, DC: Congressional Quarterly.

Orren, G. R. 1985. The nomination process: Vicissitudes of candidate selection. In Nelson, M. (Ed.), *The elections of 1984* (pp. 27–82). Washington, DC: Congressional Quarterly.

Owen, D. 1991. *Media messages in American presidential elections.* New York: Greenwood Press.

Page, B. 1978. *Choices and echoes in presidential elections.* Chicago: University of Chicago Press.

Paletz, D. L., and Guthrie, K. K. 1987. Three faces of Ronald Reagan. *Journal of Communication, 37,* 7–23.

Patterson, T. E. 1980. *The mass media election: How Americans choose their president.* New York: Praeger.

Patterson, T. E., and McClure, R. D. 1976. *The unseeing eye: The myth of television power in national elections.* New York: G. P. Putnam's Sons.

Payne, J. G., Golden, J. L., Marlier, J., and Ratzan, S. C. 1989. Perceptions of the 1988 presidential and vice-presidential debates. *American Behavioral Scientist, 32*, 425–35.

Perse, E. M., and Rubin, R. B. 1989. Attribution in social and parasocial relationships. *Communication Research, 16*, 59–77.

Petty, G. R., Kraus, S., and Chang, T. June 1990. *Viewing televised presidential debates as just another form of supporting competition: Debate viewing, campaign information and political identity.* Paper presented at the International Communcation Association Convention, Dublin, Ireland.

Petty, R. E., and Cacioppo, J. T. 1984. The effects of involvement on responses to argument quantity and quality: Central and peripheral routes to persuasion. *Journal of Personality and Social Psychology, 46*, 69–81.

Petty, R. E., Cacioppo, J. T., and Goldman, R. 1981. Personal involvement as a determinant of argument based persuasion. *Journal of Personality and Social Psychology, 41*, 847–855.

Petty, R. E., Cacioppo, J. T., and Kasmer, J. A. 1988. The role of affect in the elaboration likelihood model of persuasion. In Donohew, L., Sypher, H. E., and Higgins, E. T. (Eds.), *Communication, social cognition, and affect* (pp. 117–46). Hillsdale, NJ: Lawrence Erlbaum Associates.

Petty, R. E., Cacioppo, J. T., and Schumann, D. 1983. Central and peripheral routes to advertising effectiveness: The moderating role of involvement. *Journal of Consumer Research, 14*, 687–97.

Pfau, M. November 1983. *Political debate formats: The next step.* Paper presented at the Speech Communication Association Convention, Washington, DC.

Pfau, M. 1984. A comparative assessment of intraparty political debate formats. *Political Communication Review, 9*, 1–23.

Pfau, M. 1987. The influence of intraparty political debates on candidate preference. *Communication Research, 14*, 687–97.

Pfau, M. 1988. Intraparty political debates and issue learning. *Journal of Applied Communication Research, 16*, 99–112.

Pfau, M. 1990. A channel approach to television influence. *Journal of Broadcasting & Electronic Media, 34*, 195–214.

Pfau, M., and Burgoon, M. 1989. The efficacy of issue and character attack message strategies in political campaign communication. *Communication Reports, 2*, 53–61.

Pfau, M., and Kang, J. G. November 1989. *The impact of relational and nonverbal communication in political debate influence.* Paper presented at the Speech Communication Association Convention, San Francisco, CA.

Pfau, M., and Kenski, H. C. 1990. *Attack politics: Strategy and defense.* New York: Praeger.

Pfau, M., Kenski, H. C., Nitz, M., and Sorenson, J. November 1989. *Use of the attack message strategy in political campaign communication.* Paper presented at the Speech Communication Association Convention, San Francisco, CA.

Philpott, J. S. 1983. *The relative contribution to meaning of verbal and nonverbal channels of communication: A meta-analysis.* Master's thesis, University of Nebraska, Lincoln.

Pierce, J. C., and Sullivan, J. L. 1980. *The electorate reconsidered.* Beverly Hills, CA: Sage.

Polisky, J. B. 1965. *The Kennedy-Nixon debates: A study in political persuasion.* Ph.D. diss., University of Wisconsin-Madison.

Polsby, N. W. 1979. Debatable thoughts on presidential debates. In Ranney, A. (Ed.), *The past and future of presidential debates* (pp. 175–86). Washington, DC: American Enterprise Institute for Public Policy Research.

Pomper, G. M. 1972. From confusion to clarity: Issues and American voters, 1956–1968. *American Political Science Review, 66,* 415–28.

Pomper, G. M. 1975. *Voter's choice: Varieties of American electoral behavior.* New York: Harper & Row.

Postman, N. 1988. Critical thinking in the electronic era. In Govier, T. (Ed.), *Selected issues in logic and communication* (pp. 11–19). Belmont, CA: Wadsworth.

Prentice, D. B. November 1988. *The Commission on Presidential Debates: A new approach to political debates or just a new sponsor?* Paper presented at the Speech Communication Association convention. New Orleans, LA.

Prentice, D. B., Larsen, J. K., and Sobnosky, M. J. November 1981. *The Carter-Reagan debate: The impact of the debate format on the candidates' responsiveness and clash.* Paper presented at the Speech Communication Association Convention, Anaheim, CA.

Raines, H. October 21, 1984. New events spice already-hot debate. *Arizona Daily Star,* pp. 1, 3A.

Ranney, A. 1983. *Channels of power: The impact of television on American politics.* New York: Basic Books.

Ray, R. F. 1961. Thomas E. Dewey: The great Oregon debate of 1948. In Reid, L. (Ed.), *American public address* (pp. 247–67). Columbia: University of Missouri Press.

Reagan and the age issue. October 22, 1984. *Newsweek,* p. 26.

Reinsch, J. L. 1988. *Getting elected: From radio and Roosevelt to television and Reagan.* New York: Hippocrene Books.

Repass, D. E. 1971. Issue salience and party choice. *American Political Science Review, 65,* 389–400.

Rhine, R. J., and Severance, L. J. 1970. Ego involvement, discrepancy, source credibility and attitude change. *Journal of Personality and Social Psychology, 16,* 175–90.

Riley, P., and Hollihan, T. A. 1981. The 1980 presidential debates: A content analysis of the issues and arguments. *Speaker and Gavel, 18,* 47–59.

Riley, P., Hollihan, T., and Cooley, D. April 1980. *The 1976 presidential debates: An analysis of the issues and arguments.* Paper presented at the Central States Speech Association Convention, Chicago, IL.

Ritter, K., and Gibson, J. February 1981. *The quality of the 1980 presidential forums: A "revisionist" position on presidential debates.* Paper presented at the Western Speech Communication Association Convention, San Jose, CA.

Ritter, K., and Hellweg, S. A. May 1984. *Influence on presidential campaign debating: The incumbency factor.* Paper presented at the International Communication Association Convention, San Francisco, CA.

Ritter, K., and Hellweg, S. A. 1986. The emergence of a new national forum for political debating: Televised presidential primary debates, 1956–1984. *Journal of the American Forensic Association, 23,* 1–14.

Ritter, K., and Henry, D. 1990. The 1980 Reagan-Carter presidential debate. In Friedenberg, R. V. (Ed.), *Rhetorical studies of national political debates* (pp. 69–94). New York: Praeger.

Roberts, C. L. 1979. Media use and difficulty of decision in the 1976 presidential campaign. *Journalism Quarterly, 56,* 794–802.

Robinson, J. P. 1979. The polls. In Kraus, S. (Ed.), *The great debates: Carter vs. Ford, 1976* (pp. 262–68). Bloomington: Indiana University Press.

Robinson, M. 1978. Television and American politics: 1956–1976. *The Public Interest, 48,* 3–40.

Rollins, E. J. October 9, 1988. Debate format is right when decision is a draw. *Los Angeles Times,* pp. V1–2.

Roper, B. W. September 1977. *The effects of the debates on the Carter/Ford election.* Paper presented at the American Political Science Association Convention, Washington, DC.

Roper, E. November 1960. Polling post-mortem. *Saturday Review,* pp. 10–13.

Rose, D. D. 1979. Citizen uses of the Ford-Carter debates. *Journal of Politics, 41,* 214–21.

Rosenberg, S. W., Bohan, L., McCafferty, P., and Harris, K. 1986. The image and vote: The effect of candidate presentation on voter preference. *American Journal of Political Science, 30,* 108–27.

Rosenberg, W. W., and McCafferty, P. 1987. The image and the vote: Manipulating voter's preferences. *Public Opinion Quarterly, 51,* 31–47.

Rosenthal, P. I. 1963. *Ethos in the presidential campaign of 1960: A study of the basic persuasive process of the Kennedy-Nixon television debates.* Ph.D. diss., University of California at Los Angeles.

Rouner, D., and Perloff, R. M. May 1986. *Through the selective eyes of the political beholder: Perceptions of the 1984 presidential debate.* Paper presented at the International Communication Association Convention, Chicago, IL.

Rowland, R. 1986. The substance of the 1980 Carter-Reagan debate. *Southern Speech Communication Journal, 51,* 142–65.

Rubin, R. B., and McHugh, M. P. 1987. Development of parasocial interaction relationships. *Journal of Broadcasting & Electronic Media, 31,* 279–92.

Rudd, R. 1986. Issues as image in political campaign commercials. *Western Journal of Speech Communication, 50,* 102–18.

Ruesch, J., and Bateson, G. 1951. *Communication: The social matrix of psychiatry.* New York: W. W. Norton & Company.

Ryan, H. R. 1990. The 1988 Bush-Dukakis presidential debates. In Friedenberg, R. V. (Ed.), *Rhetorical studies of national political debates* (pp. 145–66). New York: Praeger.

Saikowski, C. October 23, 1984. Experts doubt debate will lift Mondale. *Christian Science Monitor,* pp. 1, 8.

Salomon, G. 1979. *Interaction of media, cognition, and learning.* San Francisco, CA: Jossey-Bass.

Salomon, G. 1981. *Communication and education: Social and psychological interactions.* Beverly Hills, CA: Sage.

Salomon, G. 1987. *Interaction of media, cognition and learning: An exploration of how symbolic forms cultivate mental skills and affect knowledge acquisition.* San Francisco: Jossey-Bass.

Samovar, L. A. 1962. Ambiguity and unequivocation in the Kennedy-Nixon television debates. *Quarterly Journal of Speech, 48*, 277–79.

Samovar, L. A. 1965. Ambiguity and unequivocation in the Kennedy-Nixon debates: A rhetorical analysis. *Western Speech, 29*, 211–18.

Sanders, K. R., Kimsey, W. D., and Hantz, A. M. March 1977. *The uses of the 1976 presidential debates in electoral decision making.* Paper presented at the Eastern Communication Association Convention, New York, NY.

Sauter, K. 1990. The 1976 Mondale-Dole vice-presidential debate. In Friedenberg, R. V. (Ed.), *Rhetorical studies of national political debates* (pp. 45–68). New York: Praeger.

Schram, M. 1987. *The great American video game: Presidential politics in the television age.* New York: William Morrow & Company.

Schroeder, A. December 1989. *Reforms in presidential debates: A summary of what has been tried and proposed.* Paper presented at the Conference on Presidential Debates, Washington, DC.

Scott, R. L. 1981. You cannot not debate: The debate over the 1980 presidential debates. *Speaker and Gavel, 18*, 28–33.

Sears, D. O., and Chaffee, S. H. 1979. Uses and effects of the 1976 debates: An overview of empirical studies. In Kraus, S. (Ed.), *The great debates: Carter vs. Ford, 1976* (pp. 223–61). Bloomington: Indiana University Press.

Sebald, H. 1962. Limitations of communication: mechanisms of image maintenance in the form of selective perception, selective memory, and selective distortion. *Journal of Communication, 12*, 142–49.

Seltz, H. A., and Yoakam, R. D. 1977. Production diary of the debates. In Kraus, S. (Ed.), *The great debates: Kennedy vs. Nixon, 1960* (pp. 73–126). Bloomington: Indiana University Press.

Shapiro, M. J. 1969. Rational political man: A synthesis of economic and social-psychological perpectives. *American Political Science Review, 63*, 1106–19.

Sharbutt, J. October 12, 1988. Rather declines nomination to debate panel. *Los Angeles Times*, p. I11.

Shaw, D. L., and McCombs, M. E. 1977. *The emergence of American political issues: The agenda setting function of the press.* St. Paul, MN: West Publishing Company.

Sheingold, C. A. 1973. Social networks and voting: The resurrection of a research agenda. *American Sociological Review, 38*, 712–20.

Sherman, R. N. 1966. An objective analysis of language choice in the first Nixon-Kennedy debate (Ph.D. diss., University of Michigan, 1965). *Dissertation Abstracts International, 27*, 549A.

Siepmann, C. A. 1977. Were they "great"? In Kraus, S. (Ed.), *The great debates: Kennedy vs. Nixon, 1960* (pp. 132–41). Bloomington: Indiana University Press.

Sigelman, L., and Sigelman, C. K. 1984. Judgments of the Carter-Reagan debate: The eyes of the beholder. *Public Opinion Quarterly, 48*, 624–28.

Sillars, A. L., Pike, G. R., Jones, T. S., and Murphy, M. A. 1984. Communication and understanding in marriage. *Human Communication Research, 10*, 317–50.

Simons, H. W., and Liebowitz, K. 1979. Shifts in candidate images. In Kraus, S. (Ed.), *The great debates: Carter vs. Ford, 1976* (pp. 398–404). Bloomington: Indiana University Press.

Smith, C. A., and Smith, K. B. 1990. The 1984 Reagan-Mondale presidential debates. In Friedenberg, R. V. (Ed.), *Rhetorical studies of national political debates* (pp. 95–120). New York: Praeger.

Smith, H. October 30, 1980. Carter and Reagan voicing confidence on debate showing: Performances rate close. *New York Times*, pp. A1 & B15.

Smith, R. G. 1977. The Carter-Ford debates: Some perceptions from academe. *Central States Speech Journal*, *28*, 250–57.

Steeper, F. T. 1980. Public response to Gerald Ford's statements on Eastern Europe in the second debate. In Bishop, G. F., Meadow, R. G., and Jackson-Beeck, M. (Eds.), *The presidential debates: Media, electoral, and policy perspectives* (pp. 81–101). New York: Praeger.

Stelzner, H. G. 1971. Humphrey and Kennedy court West Virginia, May 3, 1960. *Southern Speech Communication Journal*, *37*, 21–33.

Strouse, J. C. 1975. *The mass media, public opinion, and public policy analysis.* Columbus, OH: Charles E. Merrill Publishing Co.

Sullivan, P. A. 1989. The 1984 vice-presidential debate: A case study of female and male framing in political campaigns. *Communication Quarterly, 37,* 329–43.

Swanson, D. L. 1977. And that's the way it was? Television covers the 1976 presidential campaign. *Quarterly Journal of Speech, 63,* 239–48.

Swanson, L. L., and Swanson, D. L. 1978. The agenda-setting function of the first Ford-Carter debate. *Communication Monographs, 45,* 347–53.

Swerdlow, J. L. 1984. *Beyond debate: A paper on televised presidential debates.* New York: Twentieth Century Fund.

Swerdlow, J. L. 1988. The strange—and sometimes surprising—history of presidential debates in America. In Swerdlow, J. L. (Ed.), *Presidential debates: 1988 and beyond* (pp. 3–16). Washington, DC: Congressional Quarterly.

Tannenbaum, P. H., Greenberg, B. S., and Silverman, F. R. 1977. Candidate images. In Kraus, S. (Ed.), *The great debates: Kennedy vs. Nixon, 1960* (pp. 271–88). Bloomington: Indiana University Press.

Tiemens, R. K. 1978. Television's portrayal of the 1976 presidential debates: An analysis of visual content. *Communication Monographs, 45,* 362–70.

Tiemens, R. K., Hellweg, S. A., Kipper, P., and Phillips, S. L. 1985. An integrative verbal and visual analysis of the Carter-Reagan debate. *Communication Quarterly, 33,* 34–42.

Trent, J. S. 1990. The 1984 Bush-Ferraro vice presidential debate. In Friedenberg, R. V. (Ed.), *Rhetorical studies of national political debates* (pp. 121–44). New York: Praeger.

Trent, J. S., and Friedenberg, R. V. 1983. *Political campaign communication: Principles and practices.* New York: Praeger.

Twentieth Century Fund Task Force on Televised Presidential Debates. 1979. *With the nation watching: Report of the Twentieth Century Fund Task Force on Televised Presidential Debates.* Lexington, MA: D. C. Heath & Company.

Two candidates foil Demo TV debate. March 15, 1972. *Variety,* p. 36.

Vancil, D. L., and Pendell, S. D. 1984. Winning presidential debates: An analysis of criteria influencing audience response. *Western Journal of Speech Communication, 48,* 62–74.

Vancil, D. L., and Pendell, S. D. 1987. The myth of viewer listener disagreement in the first Kennedy-Nixon debate. *Central States Speech Journal, 38,* 16–27.

Vatz, R. E., Weinberg, L. S., Rabin, R., and Shipman, I. 1976. The vice-presidential debate and the theories of Paul I. Rosenthal. *Extasis, 3,* 16–23.

Wagner, J. 1983. Media do make a difference: The differential impact of mass media in the 1976 presidential race. *American Journal of Political Science, 27,* 407–30.

Wald, K. D., and Lupfer, M. B. 1978. The presidential debate as a civics lesson. *Public Opinion Quarterly, 42,* 342–53.

Walker, J. R., and Peterson, D. S. November 1981. *Image changers and presidential debates.* Paper presented at the Speech Communication Association Convention, Anaheim, CA.

Warshaw, P. R. 1978. Application of selective attention theory to television advertising displays. *Journal of Applied Psychology, 63,* 366–72.

Watzlawick, P., Beavin, J. H., and Jackson, D. D. 1967. *Pragmatics of human communication: A study of interactional patterns, pathologies, and paradoxes.* New York: W. W. Norton.

Weaver, D. H., Graber, D. A., McCombs, M. E., and Eyal, C. H. 1981. *Media agenda-setting in a presidential election: Issues, images, and interest.* New York: Praeger.

Weaver, P. H. August 29, 1976. Captives of melodrama. *New York Times Magazine,* pp. 6, 48.

Weiler, M. 1989. The 1988 electoral debates and debate theory. *Argumentation and Advocacy, 25,* 214–19.

Weintraub, B. October 8, 1984. Reagan debates Mondale in first of two meetings. *New York Times,* pp. 1, 11.

Weisberg, H. F., and Rusk, J. G. 1970. Dimensions of candidate evaluation. *American Political Science Review, 64,* 1167–85.

Weiss, R. O. 1981. The presidential debates in their political context: The issue-image interface in the 1980 campaign. *Speaker and Gavel, 18,* 22–27.

White, T. 1982. *America in search of itself: The making of the president 1956–1980.* New York: Harper & Row.

White, T. 1961. *The making of the president 1960.* New York: Atheneum.

Williams, D. C., Weber, S. J., Haaland, G. A., Mueller, R. H., and Craig, R. E. 1976. Voter decisionmaking in a primary election: An evaluation of three models of choice. *American Journal of Political Science, 20,* 37–49.

Windt, T. O. 1990. The 1960 Kennedy-Nixon presidential debate. In Friedenberg, R. V. (Ed.), *Rhetorical studies in national political debates* (pp. 1–27). New York: Praeger.

Wingerson, L. March 1982. Nice guys finish first: A study of facial politics concludes that a candidate should not lead with his chin. *Discover,* pp. 66–67.

Witcover, J. March 6, 1972. Muskie, McGovern clash on finances: Debate over disclosing sources dominates 5-candidate TV panel. *Los Angeles Times,* sec. 1, p. 1.

Wright, P. L. 1974. Analyzing media effects on advertising responses. *Public Opinion Quarterly, 38,* 192–205.

Zapple, N. 1979. Historical evaluation of section 315. In Ranney, A. (Ed.), *The past and future of presidential debates* (pp. 56–69). Washington, DC: American Enterprise Institute for Public Policy Research.

Author Index

Subject Index

About the Authors

SUSAN A. HELLWEG is a Professor in the Department of Speech Communication at San Diego State University. She has published more than forty articles, chapters, and monographs, her work appearing in such journals as *Central States Speech Journal*, *Communication Quarterly*, *Communication Reports*, *Journal of the American Forensic Association*, *Journal of Business Communication*, *Management Communication Quarterly*, *Public Productivity Review*, *Southern Speech Communication Journal*, and *Speaker and Gavel*. She currently serves on the editorial boards of *Journal of Applied Communication Research*, *Management Communication Quarterly*, and *Western Journal of Speech Communication*.

MICHAEL PFAU is Professor and Chair of the Department of Speech Communication at Augustana College, Sioux Falls, South Dakota. He has published more than thirty chapters and articles, appearing in such journals as *Argumentation and Advocacy*, *Communication Education*, *Communication Monographs*, *Communication Quarterly*, *Communication Reports*, *Communication Studies*, *Communication Research*, *Human Communication Research*, *Journal of Broadcasting & Electronic Media*, *Western Political Quarterly*, and others. He has co-authored two previous books, *Debate and Argument: A Systems Approach to Advocacy*, with David Thomas and Walter Ulrich (1987), and *Attack Politics: Strategy and Defense*, with Henry Kenski (Praeger, 1990).

STEVEN R. BRYDON is Chair and Professor in the Department of Human Communication Studies and former Chair in the Department of Journalism at California State University, Chico. He is a political analyst for KHSL-TV, a Chico television station, and has been a consultant for congressional and state legislative candidates. He has published articles in the *Central States Speech Journal, Journal of the American Forensic Association*, and *Quarterly Journal of Speech*, and is currently writing *Between One and Many: An Introduction to Public Speaking* with Michael D. Scott.